DISCOVERING
ACADIA
AN INTRODUCTION TO THE PARK AND ITS ENVIRONMENT

D1249662

BY LAURIE HOBBS-OLSON

About the Author: Laurie Hobbs-Olson holds a Bachelor of Science degree in Botany from Ohio University and a Masters in Science Education from the University of Maine. She has been a ranger-naturalist with the National Park Service for 12 years serving in seven National Park areas, most recently as Acadia's environmental education coordinator. She and her husband reside on their beloved Mount Desert Island where she tends to her children as well as a large garden.

Front Cover: Bass Harbor Head Light. Marking the entrance of Blue Hill Bay and Bass Harbor, this light has guided boats into safe harbors since it was built in 1858. Automated in 1974, it is still owned and managed by the U.S. Coast Guard. **Photo by James Randklev**

Left: Sandy beaches are uncommon along Maine's rocky coast. Acadia's Sand Beach is an even greater rarity due to its high shell content. Seventy percent of Sand Beach's sand is composed of shell fragments from intertidal creatures such as barnacles, mussels, and sea urchins. **Photo by Glenn Van Nimwegen**

Above left: Hooded seal pup. Although rare around Acadia, hooded seals have had an increase in occurrences during recent winters. **Photo by Thomas Mark Szelog**

Above right: Granite boulders carved and shaped by the tides. **Photo by David Muench**

INTRODUCTION

"Scenically, its impressive headlands give Mount Desert the distinction of combining sea and mountain... Back of the shore is a mountain and lake wilderness which is typical in a remarkable degree of the range of Appalachian scenery...There are few spots, if any, which can combine the variety and luxuriance of the eastern forests in such small compass. The rocks have their distinction... worn by the ice sheets of the glacial period, eroded by the frosts and rains of the ages, their bases carved by the sea, their surfaces painted by the mosses and lichens of today, they are exhibits of scientific interest as well as beauty. Still, another distinction is Mount Desert's wealth of bird life. All the conditions for a bird sanctuary in the east seem to be here fulfilled."

- Excerpts from a letter written in 1918 by Franklin K. Lane, Secretary of the Interior, on why this area was worthy of national park status.

Sand Beach Photo by Glenn Van Nimwegen

Off the coast of Maine lies a mountainous island, filled with forested valleys and sparkling lakes surrounded by rocky coastline and crashing surf. Mount Desert Island, home to Acadia National Park, contains an incredible array of magnificent environments, all on one island. The park also includes the remote island wilderness of Isle au Haut and the mainland Schoodic Peninsula.

It is difficult for words to truly convey Acadia's soul. Pictures help some, but the real Acadia lies within each individual's experience of the park. Somewhere, be it crouched by the side of a tidepool or immersed in the quiet of a mountain summit, will be the place that defines Acadia.

Visitors of today were not the first to be captivated by Acadia's charms. First used by prehistoric people, the more recent Wabanaki tribes knew this land as "Pemetiq," meaning "sloping land." Europeans would come to know it as "Isles des Monts Deserts," the title Samuel Champlain bestowed upon this island with barren mountain tops. Once the British and French ceased quarreling over domain of the region, colonization of the island began in earnest. Beginning in the mid-1800's, people lured by the scenic landscape eventually turned the island into a playground for the affluent. Some, such as Charles Eliot, George B. Dorr, and John D. Rockefeller, Jr., sought ways to protect it for all. On July 8, 1916, Sieur de Monts National Monument was designated and on February 26, 1919, Lafayette National Park was born, the first national park east of the Mississippi.

Preceding pages: The granite slopes of Cadillac Mountain cloaked in the glorious colors of autumn. From left to right can be seen Gorham Mountain, Otter Point, Otter Cove, and Hunters Head. Baker Island and Little Cranberry Island are in the distance.
Photo by James Randklev

Left: From atop South Bubble, Jordan Pond and the outlying islands of Sutton, Great Cranberry, and Little Cranberry sprawl in the background.
Photo by Carr Clifton.

Right: Acadia mountains meet the sea along the Park Loop Road. Acadia encompasses mountains, lakes, and coastline all on one island.
Photo by Carr Clifton

On January 19, 1929, it was renamed Acadia National Park.

Today the park comprises over 46,000 acres. Twenty six rounded mountains, U-shaped valleys, over 20 glacial lakes and ponds, even a fjord are a direct result of glacial carving on the hard granite bedrock. Forty-one miles of rocky coastline with pocket beaches, mud-flats, and salt marshes, are preserved. Acadia's diversity not only applies to habitat variety but in the range of plant species numbering over 1,200. Wildlife abounds from small to large with over 270 species of birds sighted.

While the primary mission of Acadia is to protect and preserve, the park also provides outstanding opportunities for recreation. Over 100 miles of hiking trails lead visitors down gentle pathways or up strenuous mountain climbs. A network of carriage roads, developed by John D. Rockefeller Jr., provide access into Acadia's heart either by foot, bike, or horse. Boat cruises, canoeing, and swimming are all ways to take advantage of the park's water resources. Ranger-led interpretive programs teach visitors about all aspects of the park.

Three million visitors a year come to Acadia, either to discover it for the first time or just because they are drawn back to its majestic beauty. Somewhere, amid mountain vistas, serene lakes, peaceful meadows, and inspired shoreline is a place that will forever create vivid memories of this island national park. Enjoy the search to capture Acadia.

GEOGRAPHY

Sailing into the sunrise. During the fall and winter, Acadia National Park is the first point to greet the rising sun in the United States. In the spring and summer, that title belongs further to the north, but only by a few minutes. Chances are if you are watching an Acadian sunrise across the Gulf of Maine, you are one of the first in the country to greet its welcoming rays.
Photo by Glenn Van Nimwegen

Preceding pages: Sunrise over Acadia's 2,000 acre Schoodic Peninsula. Egg Rock Lighthouse, Turtle Island, and Winter Harbor Lighthouse are in the foreground. Beyond Schoodic is Mount Desert Rock Lighthouse, 23 miles out to sea. Imagine life as a lighthouse keeper there !
Photo by Jeff Gnass

Left: Fog shrouds a mountain view. Fog comes in many forms, from early morning mists to winter sea smoke, to coastal fog on warm summer days. Although an integral part of Acadia's beauty, it is a different story if you are a mariner in the thick of it. Prior to modern navigational equipment, captains would inch their boats along listening for familiar sounds of land.
Photo by Fred Hirschmann

Right: The Schoodic Peninsula includes rocky headlands, island views, and the panorama of Mount Desert Island.
Photo by Willard Clay

Located on 80,000 acre Mount Desert Island, Acadia National Park is mid-way along the coast of Maine. Mount Desert Island, the third largest East Coast island, behind Long Island and Martha's Vineyard, is shaped like a lobster claw. Dividing the east and west portions of this 18 mile long island is Somes Sound, the only *"fjord"* on the East Coast. The island's rounded mountainous topography, drowned coastline, and lakes are a direct result of glacial carving. Flanking the island's steep granite cliffs is Frenchman Bay to the east and Blue Hill Bay to the west. The park shares the island with four communities: Bar Harbor, Southwest Harbor, Northeast Harbor, and Bass Harbor, as well as smaller villages.

Acadia comprises about one third of Mount Desert Island preserving over 30,000 acres of coniferous and deciduous forests, dotted with streams, meadows, and peatlands. Coarse-grained pink granite mountains span the island's 14 mile width. Acadia has 26 mountains with 8 mountains reaching heights over 1,000 feet. Cadillac Mountain at 1,530 feet, is the highest mountain along the eastern seaboard. From atop Cadillac's well-visited summit, the panorama encompassing Acadia's incredible diversity of lake and pond shores, marshes and coastline, mountain tops and forest floors, stretches in all directions. Islands, such as Acadia's Porcupines and Baker, dot the ocean.

This remarkable variety of environments on one single island translates to wildlife diversity. Close to 300 species of birds temporarily visit, or breed in Acadia. Over 40 different mammals, 11 amphibians, 7 reptiles, a large number of insects and invertebrates, all sur-

rounded by a strand of ocean and tidepool creatures, round out the rich menagerie.

Acadia's plants also illustrate this diversity. The area's maritime environment of fog and humidity, cooler growing seasons and warmer winters, all influenced by the proximity to the Gulf of Maine, sustain a variety of northern and southern plants that represent a range of over 2,500 miles. Many of these species meet side by side. There are very few areas with this combination of arctic, Canadian zone, and southern coastal plain plants all in one geographical location. For example, on Acadia Mountain, pitch pine and bear oak, both common to New Jersey coastal plains, are found growing next to black crowberry, a Canadian resident. The mixing of northern and southern plants is certainly not the only aspect of Acadia's diversity. Many of its landmarks are deemed worthy of special protection because of their natural, scientific, scenic, or historical values. Fourteen areas in Acadia are registered as Maine State Critical Areas for preservation. They include Sand Beach, two stands of old growth forests, habitats with rare and endangered plants, unique forest stands, and park peatlands.

To the northeast of Mount Desert Island, the long granite finger of Schoodic Peninsula forms the eastern boundary of Frenchman Bay. Two thousand acres of this peninsula, acquired in 1929, belong to Acadia National Park. Approximately a 1-hour drive north of Mount Desert Island, Schoodic's five mile, one-way scenic drive hugs the coast, providing long-distance views of Mount Desert Island's mountains and intimate looks of what the

Maine coast has to offer: rocky cliffs, tide pools, islands, and mud flats. The road winds around the base of Schoodic Mountain. For a view from the top, a dirt road and hiking trails access the summit. During ocean storms this area displays spectacular surf. As ocean swells slam into the granite headlands, geyser after geyser shoots into the air. These granite slabs also exhibit some outstanding geologic features. Thick, long, black basaltic dikes bisect the bedrock.

On Mount Desert Island's western horizon, Isle au Haut's single mountain stands behind a spattering of smaller islands. Named by Champlain in 1604, it means "high island" in French. Half of Isle au Haut is part of Acadia National Park. Eighteen miles of rugged trails traverse this island with its high bluffs, freshwater lake, and deep spruce forests with streams, marshes, and bogs. This part of Acadia is only accessible by mailboat from Stonington, ME, a 1 ½-hour drive from Mount Desert Island.

Diversity certainly applies to all aspects of Acadia's climate with July's cool sea breezes, November's thundering surf, or January's ice-coated trees. The Gulf of Maine's influence results in a slow spring warm-up and cool summer temperatures, but allows for warmer autumns and milder winters. This minor temperature difference occurs because a large body of water such as the Gulf warms slower than land, yet holds on to that relative warmth long into the winter. That "warm" temperature only reaches a 55 degree average in August.

Fog is an integral part of the beauty of the Acadia coast, softening edges with shrouded mist while framing close up views rather than distant vistas. There are many different types of fogs, each enhancing its own Acadian mood. Fog can be created by a variety of conditions such as rainy weather, daily temperature changes, or geography. Radiation fog is created from the cooling of a land-based air mass, occurring early in the morning or late in the evening. Sea smoke, wisps of floating fog, is common on very cold, clear winter morn-

ings. This occurs when the surface of the ocean's warmer waters clash with the cold air mass, evaporating water into the air. The reverse happens in the summer, when warm air hits the cooler air over the ocean. A sunny morning at Bubble Pond does not guarantee the same along the coast. Sometimes, during the summer, the island's edge is socked in with fog. From atop Cadillac Mountain, one can watch the fog form, billow over, then blanket the outer islands, eventually enveloping the coast.

Just as fog is a part of Acadia's essence, so are seasonal changes. The approach of spring is heralded two ways: by the change in light and the arrival of birds. As February draws to a close, the light changes, becoming stronger and lasting longer. The early migrants arrive by March's end, and bird by bird their songs are added. By the time May has arrived the chorus is in full swing.

Although spring warms slowly and snow is not uncommon in April, rain is frequent. Slowly, the gray silhouettes of the trees become awash in color. Patches of red from maple flowers, the bright green of budding leaves, and the white flowers of shadbush trees sweep across the mountain slopes. Autumn may be the obvious time for brilliant colors, but spring brings its own palette, although more subdued. Among the last trees to leaf out are the red oaks, slowly unfurling their leaves like small tentative hands. With the trees fully dressed in their new greenery, summer is underway with daytime temperatures in the 70's and 80's and nighttime lows in the 50's.

Sunrise watching on Cadillac is a popular activity for early risers who wake by 4:00 a.m. to catch the early rays. Will they be the first in the United States to greet the sunrise? Perhaps, depending on the time of year. Because of the yearly swings in sunrise, different spots along the Maine coast will see sunrise first. In the summer, it rises north of east, in the winter, it rises south of east. Cadillac Mountain is the site for the first sunrise from October 7 to March 6. From

ISLE AU HAUT

About half of Isle au Haut, French for "high island," belongs to Acadia National Park. The island, about 15 miles southwest of Mount Desert Island, is only accessible by mailboat from Stonington. A limited amount of day visitors and campers with pre-arranged camping reservations for five lean-to shelters may visit this remote portion of Acadia.

SCHOODIC PENINSULA

A 2,000 acre tract on Schoodic Peninsula belongs to Acadia National Park. Easily accessible, its five-mile scenic road offers the visitor unobstructed views of Mount Desert Island across Frenchman Bay. Its shores, providing cobblestone beaches, rocky ledges, bays, and mountain sights, are some of the more picturesque in Maine.

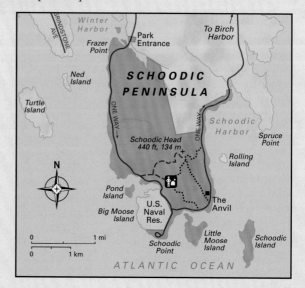

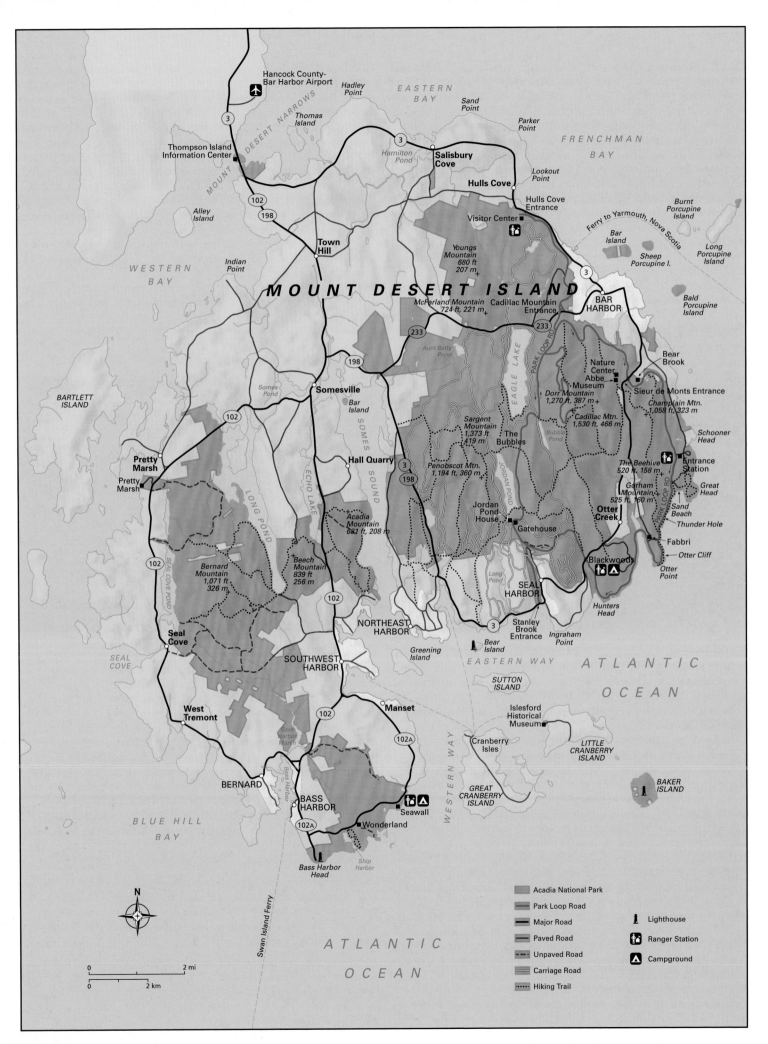

Hancock County-
Bar Harbor Airport

*Hadley
Point*

*EASTERN
BAY*

*Sand
Point*

*Parker
Point*

*FRENCHMAN
BAY*

Thompson Island
Information Center

*Thomas
Island*

**Salisbury
Cove**

*Hamilton
Pond*

Hulls Cove

*Lookout
Point*

Hulls Cove
Entrance

Ferry to Yarmouth, Nova Scotia

*Burnt
Porcupine
Island*

*Bar
Island*

*Long
Porcupine
Island*

Visitor Center

*Bald
Porcupine
Island*

*WESTERN
BAY*

*Alley
Island*

**Town
Hill**

*Indian
Point*

MOUNT DESERT ISLAND

*Youngs
Mountain
680 ft
207 m*

*McFarland Mountain
724 ft, 221 m*

Cadillac Mountain
Entrance

**BAR
HARBOR**

*Sheep
Porcupine I.*

*BARTLETT
ISLAND*

*Somes
Pond*

Somesville

Bar Island

*Aunt Betty
Pond*

*EAGLE
LAKE*

Nature
Center
Abbe
Museum

*Bear
Brook*

Sieur de Monts Entrance

*Dorr Mountain
1,270 ft, 387 m*

*Champlain Mtn.
1,058 ft, 323 m*

*Sargent
Mountain
1,373 ft
419 m*

*The
Bubbles*

*Bubble
Pond*

*Cadillac Mtn.
1,530 ft, 466 m*

*Schooner
Head*

**Pretty
Marsh**

*Pretty
Marsh*

Hall Quarry

*Penobscot Mtn.
1,194 ft, 360 m*

*The Beehive
520 ft, 158 m*

Entrance
Station

*Great
Head*

*Acadia
Mountain
681 ft, 208 m*

*Jordan
Pond*

Jordan
Pond
House

*Gorham
Mountain
525 ft, 160 m*

*Sand
Beach*

Gatehouse

Thunder Hole

**Otter
Creek**

*Bernard
Mountain
1,071 ft
326 m*

*Beech
Mountain
839 ft
256 m*

*Long
Pond*

Fabbri

Otter Cliff

Blackwoods

**SEAL
HARBOR**

*Otter
Point*

**Seal
Cove**

**NORTHEAST
HARBOR**

*Hunters
Head*

*SEAL
COVE*

Stanley
Brook
Entrance

*Ingraham
Point*

**West
Tremont**

**SOUTHWEST
HARBOR**

*Greening
Island*

Bear Island

EASTERN WAY

ATLANTIC

Manset

*SUTTON
ISLAND*

OCEAN

Islesford
Historical
Museum

*LITTLE
CRANBERRY
ISLAND*

BERNARD

*Bass Harbor
Marsh*

Cranberry
Isles

WESTERN WAY

*BAKER
ISLAND*

**BASS
HARBOR**

Seawall

Wonderland

*GREAT
CRANBERRY
ISLAND*

*BLUE HILL
BAY*

*Bass Harbor
Head*

*Ship
Harbor*

Swan Island Ferry

N

ATLANTIC

OCEAN

	Acadia National Park
	Park Loop Road
	Major Road
	Paved Road
	Unpaved Road
	Carriage Road
	Hiking Trail

Lighthouse

Ranger Station

Campground

0   2 mi

0   2 km

March 25 through September 18, the sunrise belongs to Mars Hill in northern Maine. The two weeks around the spring and autumn equinoxes, it rises first at Quoddy Head, also to the north.

Sunsets are perhaps more popular and Cadillac's granite ledges fill with visitors looking across Eagle Lake towards Blue Hill, a dominant bump on the western horizon. Streaks of pink and orange cut through the azure sky as the sun dips below the horizon. At times during the summer, however, that view of Blue Hill becomes a vague gray shape, obscured in part by pollutant particulate matter. Like other national parks, Acadia is not isolated from poor air quality. Occasionally, summer ground level ozone levels exceed safe health standards. Ground level ozone, unlike the earth's protective ozone layer, is a by-product pollutant from the chemical reaction of nitrogen oxides in combination with sunlight. These pollutants, primarily from fossil fuel combustion, are transported from Northeast coast cities and Midwest industrial areas to the Maine coast by the prevailing winds. These winds flow

chlorophyll dies, other pigments already present in the leaves take center stage. Hints of this spectacular change of color appear first in the birches as they acquire a yellowish tinge. By the end of September, the show is underway with peak foliage usually reached during the first two weeks of October. Red maples in swampy areas turn scarlet; aspens and beech turn golden; sugar maples become a spectacular mix of orange, yellow, and brilliant red. The tamarack's deciduous needles turn a dusty yellow. Among the last trees to turn are the red oaks, their deep burgundy and gold leaves eventually turning to brown. Late October and November often bring storms which strip the trees of their remaining leaves, signaling the end of autumn and the advent of winter.

Winter, when the trees hang with the white icing of snow or crystals of ice, is magical. Although the average snowfall is 60 inches, barren ground is just as common. Snowstorms can be followed by rainstorms, given the milder nature of the coastline. Daytime temperatures are generally in the teens and twenty's, but

northeast, heading along the "downeast" coast. Given the appropriate summer conditions of longer daylight hours and higher temperatures, the chemical reaction creating ozone has occurred by the time it reaches the coast. Fine particulates associated with this pollutant bath create visibility so poor that at times long distance views are completely lost.

Acid precipitation is also a concern. Acadia's average rainfall pH is 4.6, about five times more acidic than normal. Much of the acid precipitation-contributing pollutants, sulfur dioxide and nitrogen oxides, come from the Central and Upper Midwest. Acid precipitation contributes to greater stress in plants, hindering growth and potentially resulting in death. In aquatic systems, pH levels could drop, increasing acidity levels and leading to ecological imbalances that affect many organisms. Although it appears that most of Acadia's lakes and ponds are currently capable of buffering the acid precipitation, it is unknown if those capacities are being stretched to their limits.

Summer's approaching end is often heralded around mid-August. Goldenrod line the roadways. The air turns crisper and the shadows grow longer as days shorten. From the mountain summits, visitors can watch the migration progression of squadrons of hawks. Two of the best vantage points for observing broad-winged hawks, kestrals, sharp-shinned hawks, and golden eagles trek to the south are Beech and Cadillac Mountain. Some counts in a single afternoon have been as high as 600 birds!

Shorter days and cooler temperatures trigger trees to stop production of chlorophyll. As photosynthesis slows, and the green

bitter cold temperatures below zero are not uncommon. During a snowy winter, cross-country skiing on the park's carriage roads is popular. If there is little snow, than ice skating on glass-smooth lakes and ponds takes precedent. Frosty clear cold mornings bring wisps of sea smoke rising from the oceans.

Wildlife can be spotted, as deer browse along cedar branches, or the now white snowshoe hare nibbles on buds above the snow pack. The *dee-dee-dee* of the black-capped chickadee clearly rings through ice blue skies. Rafts of eider ducks are commonly seen on the winter ocean. Scoters, oldsquaws, and goldeneyes overwinter here and may be observed around Thompson and Bar Island.

The park remains open for those well prepared to handle the cold temperatures and short daylight hours, although the Park Loop Road remains mostly closed. A 2-mile stretch along the ocean and access to Jordan Pond are available for driving, as is Sargent Drive.

Above: Sunrise over granite formations and barnacles at low tide in the Wonderland area. Wonderland is just southwest of Southwest Harbor past Seawall. Low tide provides the casual observer with an entire new world to discover. Barnacles, abundant around Acadia's coastline, are related to the lobster, crab, and shrimp.
Photo by Hardie Truesdale

Right: A view of Cadillac Mountain and Mount Desert Island across Frenchman Bay taken from Schoodic Peninsula. The highest point on the Eastern Seaboard with an altitude of 1,530 feet, Cadillac Mountain can be seen from many miles out at sea.
Photo by William H. Johnson

GEOLOGY

Acadia's geologic "pages" are an open book for those who wish to read it. Etched in the exposed metamorphic, sedimentary, and igneous rocks are the stories of ancient seas and mountains, of continents on the move, of weathering, deposition, and ice.

Although geologists believe the earth is 4.6 billion years old, Acadia's text begins approximately 500 million years ago. The park's oldest rocks, Ellsworth Schist, are visible along the island's northwestern edge. Accumulations of sediments on an ancient sea floor were the beginnings of this *metamorphic rock*. Buried several miles below the earth's surface, the extreme heat and pressure metamorphosed these sedimentary layers, creating a compressed rock with strong foliation. Its platy appearance is predominantly gray, but greenish chlorite, quartz, and feldspar are obvious upon closer inspection.

Another area of exposed bedrock was formed in a shallow sea over 400 million years ago. The Bar Harbor formation, so named since outcroppings are mostly found in that vicinity, is a *sedimentary rock* composed of sandstone and mudstone. The brownish gray-purple or greenish rock layers tilt gently.

Following the accumulation of Bar Harbor formation sediments on the sea floor, explosive volcanic eruptions belched tons of ash and rock fragments into the air. An ashy-gray *igneous rock* with small embedded particles resulted. Named for the primary exposure on the Cranberry Isles, the Cranberry Isle formation is also found on the southwestern edge of the island around Seawall.

One of the better known sites of the park, this massive granite rock was left behind by retreating ice sheets. The size of a small van, Bubble Rock, seems to cling precariously to the side of South Bubble Mountain. The rock's large black and white crystals are foreign to Mount Desert Island. This particular glacial "erratic," a name for rocks that have been pushed or transported by moving glaciers, originated 15 miles to the northwest of Acadia.
Photo by William H. Johnson

These three rock types partially circle the island's edge. Although interesting in their formation, visitors do not flock to Acadia to view them in particular. Another geologic event was responsible for creating the park's beautiful backdrop and for drawing millions of visitors in search of its sights. The heart of Acadia belongs to coarse-grained pink granite.

Unlike the *extrusive* igneous formation of the Cranberry Isles, coarse-grained granite was formed below the surface of the earth. Igneous rock, which means born of fire, is classified as *extrusive* if it comes from an above ground source, such as a volcano, or *intrusive*, if it comes from magma below ground. Over 400 million years ago, this granite began as a pluton, a geologic term, named for the underworld god Pluto. This huge magma reservoir from the earth's mantle slowly moved up, metamorphosing or completely engulfing the rock above and along its sides. As the magma edged away from the earth's mantle, the crystallization of minerals began. The coarse-grained crystals of the granite's pink feldspar, white quartz, black hornblende, and biotite, are an indication that it cooled slowly beneath the earth.

Circling the coarse-grained granite is a semi-circle of rusty, jumbled, jagged looking rocks. This is the shatter zone, the direct result of the magma intrusion as it wedged its way through the bedrock above. The shatter zone has a wealth of minerals, created as bedrock was melted, recrystallized, and mixed with magma. Pockets of quartz, narrow veins of yellow sulfur, and green epidote run through the rock. Iron and manganese oxide stain the area red

Left: Jordan Pond is a glacially carved trough filled with glacial meltwater. The Bubbles display characteristic "plucking" of the southern mountain slopes, where ice ripped off huge chunks of rock, leaving steep-sided cliffs behind.
Photo by David Muench

Right: Granite rock formation above Thunder Hole at sunrise. Appearing impervious to the onslaught of waves, the rockbound coast is perpetually chipped away.
Photo by Jack Dykinga

and black. Chunks of bedrock that did not melt are embedded in the contorted rocks. Good places to explore the shatter zone are Otter Point and Great Head.

The granite's formation, as well as the creation of Cranberry Isle rock type, is a direct product of the continental drift theory. The volcanic source of the Cranberry Isles and the magma plug of the coarse-grained granite occurred as the Atlantic Ocean and the North

American plate fused with a now-extinct continent called Avalonia. As it began to break apart, a portion of Avalonia stuck to North America. It is believed that Ellsworth Schist was part of this ancient continent. Similar rocks to Ellsworth Schist are found along the coast of Canada and Massachusetts.

As the intense pressure under which the granite formed was released, cracks developed. Minor magma intrusions squirted through some of these larger rock fractures. These dark *diabase dikes* contrast with the pink granite. The most obvious of these are on the drive up Cadillac and at Schoodic. Granite's blocky appearance and its tendency to fracture at 90 degree angles can also be attributed to pressure release cracking. The constant exposure to freezing and thawing, rain, and wind continue to widen and change these natural cracks into wide fractures.

There are other rocks in addition to the predominant coarse-grained granite. *Gabbro* and *diorite* are two different coarse-grained igneous rocks, whose magma intruded through the rock layers. Exposed on the northwest side of the island, *gabbro* is dark while the lighter colored *diorite*, caps the Porcupines.

Other pink granites are found on the western side of Acadia. A fine-grained pink granite that intruded close to the surface is exposed on the southwestern section of the island. Its fine-grained appearance indicates that it cooled rapidly. A medium-grained pale pink granite exposed in the Somesville area displaced a portion of coarse-grained granite as it fractured. This granite in particular was sought after for buildings in the late 1800's and was used in the construction of such buildings as the U.S. Mint's first location in Philadelphia.

Hundreds of millions of years after the granite formed, glaciers shaped the land into the characteristic Acadia topography of rounded mountains, U-shaped valleys, and trough lakes. During the most recent glacial period, the great ice sheets did not cover present-day Maine until about 18,000 years ago. Deep sea cores indicate that in the past 2 to 3 million years there have been 20 to 30 glacial events. A glacial event may be caused by enough of a shift in the angle of the earth's axis to change the average world temperature by 3 to 6 degrees centigrade. More snow falls in the winter than melts in the summer. As more and more snow accumulates, underlying layers become so compacted they turn to ice. The weight of the continuing snow causes the ice to move very slowly, creeping forward a few yards a year.

The constant grinding of the ice, estimated at a mile thick in this area, sculpted the land. The east-west ridge of coarse-grained granite was rounded, plucked, and in weaker rock areas, removed altogether as the ice inched from north to south. The ice gouged out deep troughs between the mountains creating U-shaped valleys. The shape and texture of Acadia's mountains are directly related to the effect of *plucking*. Great force was exerted as the ice sheet engulfed the east-west mountainous ridge. Ice under pressure reaches its melting point and begins to turn to water. The ice sheet, literally riding on a sheet of water, creeped up and over the ridge. Having cleared the ridge, it continued to flow toward the south. Without the granite obstacle in its way, pressure was released. The water froze as fingers of ice in the fractures of the granite. As the conveyor belt of ice continued its southward progression, blocks of granite were ripped from the ridge's side and became embedded in the ice.

Above left: Granite blocking and jointing on Champlain Mountain. Granite's natural tendency to fracture at 90 degrees exaggerates with the addition of weathering and erosion.
Photo by Glenn Van Nimwegen

Above: This inlaid diorite is an example of the magma intrusion on the overlying rocks. Not completely metamorphosed, it became embedded in the shatter zone upon cooling.
Photo by Glenn Van Nimwegen

Left: Minute fractures become small fault lines as freezing and thawing work their effect over time, eroding the mountains further.
Photo by Jeff Randklev

Right: Summit of Cadillac Mountain with glacial erratics. The ice sheet that covered this area was a mile thick, equal to three Cadillac Mountains on top of each other. Upon retreat, it left rock debris strewn across Acadia.
Photo by Fred Hirschmann

GEOLOGICAL FORMATION OF ACADIA

Mount Desert Island (MDI) is the product of a series of geological events beginning 500 million years ago and culminating with the flow of glaciers up to a few thousand years ago. Because of these events all three major bedrock types can be found: *Sedimentary*, formed from layered sediments, *igneous*, formed by cooling magma, and *metamorphic*, recrystallized rock by heat and pressure.

500 Million Years Ago (MYA): Mud and sediments accumulated on an ocean floor. Through heat and pressure rock was formed.

420-360 MYA: A continent called Avalonia collided with N. America. *Folding* and *metamorphism* of rocks resulted. Heat and magma *intrusion*.

245-1.6 MYA: Drifting apart of continents and slow creation of Atlantic Ocean. Mountains eroded into an east-west ridge in MDI area.

2.4 MYA: Glaciation begins. A series of southward-moving, mile-thick glaciers have covered, and eroded the area.

To 21,000 YA: By *abrasion* and *plucking* the most recent glaciers eroded the area forming U-shaped valleys, a fjord, and *roches moutonnées*.

18,000 YA: Ice began to retreat northward. MDI was free of ice 12,500 years ago.

Ice melted, raising oceans and drowning the coastline. As area rose, freed from ice weight, it left MDI and its landforms as we know them today.

GLACIAL ACTION

The erosive power of a southward-moving mile-thick ice sheet shaped Acadia's mountains and nearby islands. The ice smoothed the north facing slopes and carved the south facing ones by "plucking." The shape thus created are called "Roches Moutonnées." Typical examples are The Bubbles and the Beehive. (See Text)

These scraped along the mountains, at times grinding so deep they left behind small half-moon depressions, called *chatter marks*. These can be recognized by their north-south orientation and their rounded appearance.

For a gradual climb up one of Acadia's mountains, choose the northern slope with its gentle rise, the result of the glacier gliding along a thin sheet of water. For heart pumping hikes, the southern sides with their steep-sided *plucked* cliffs, provide challenging terrain.

Through their carving motion the glaciers transported debris and rocks of all sizes. These remnants of glacial baggage are called *erratics* and are present throughout Acadia. The most famous, Bubble Rock, parked on the side of South Bubble, is the size of a mini-van and originated 15 miles to the northwest.

After reaching the continental shelf, the ice sheet began to recede. Beneath the ice, meltwater channels of raging water carved notches between Huguenot Head and Champlain, and Cadillac and Dorr. Chunks of ice left behind by the glacial retreat in the troughs became many of the lakes and ponds. One very deeply carved trough filled with sea water and became Somes Sound, the only fjord on the United States' east coast. A fjord is a steep-cliffed valley drowned by the sea and characterized by a shallower mouth and deeper end.

Sea level rose, immersing most of Mount Desert Island except for the mountain summits. Champlain and Cadillac became islands. Remnants from the old shoreline can be found around 220 feet on some of the mountain sides. Gorham Mountain's Cadillac Cliffs trail is flanked by familiar wave-carved cliffs from the shoreline below, except this shoreline is cloaked in a forest. A sea cave with rounded boulders wedged in the rock is about half-way along the trail. So why is sea level so much lower today? Actually, it is the land that rose. The weight of the ice compressed the land into the earth's mantle, but over time the land had a chance to rebound from its frozen weight, and it began to rise, perhaps even higher than it is now. Geologic records show that Frenchman Bay was dry about 6,000 years ago.

The same processes that delivered the exquisite Acadia landscape continue today as gravity takes down rocks, the sea pounds at the island's edge, and wind and rain etch away at the land.

THE LAND

Acadia has come a long way since the retreat of glacial ice, when the land was scraped and barren. Today, Acadia's mountains, valleys, and shoreline are cloaked with over 1,200 plant species, from the small bunchberry to the towering white pines. Each habitat harbors plants adapted to specific conditions: the thin acidic soils of the spruce forests, the post 1947 fire birch and aspen woods, the exposed mountain tops, and the cool climate of the coast.

The remarkable variety that is Acadia began, in part, with small pioneer plants that helped turn a post-glacial landscape of debris into the remarkable beauty that we know today. Lichens are one of the first steps in revegetation. These organisms, a symbiotic relationship between an algae and a fungus, help to hold rubble in place and to slow down erosion. Not necessarily fast growers, lichens produce an acid that breaks down rock, which in turn, provides available nutrients for succeeding stages of plants to get a foothold. That process continues today just as it did 13,000 years ago. Close inspection of a lichen "forest" reveals the variety of shapes and sizes and the characteristics that assign each species to one of three groupings. Obvious fruiting structures, such as the bright red-capped stalk of British soldiers, identify the fruticose variety. Another member, reindeer lichen, often called reindeer moss, carpets forest floors and rocky crevices. Its grayish-green spongy branches resemble reindeer antlers. Old man's beard, with its pale-green filamentous growth, defines the sometimes "nether-world" appearance of

Big tooth aspen leaves. Named for the obvious toothed leaves, both this tree and its relative, the quaking aspen, have flattened leaf stalks, causing the leaves to twist back and forth in the wind. Acadia's forests are an intricate mix of hardwood and conifers. Aspen and birch can be found in many areas on the east side where the fire of 1947 swept through. The west side of the park is dominated by red spruce and balsam fir, as is the area between Little Hunter's Beach and Jordan Pond. Mixed forests of beech, maple, oak, hemlock, white pine, and white cedar cover other park areas.
Photo by John Netherton

Preceding pages: Lifting fog in a spruce forest near Seawall and the Wonderland area. Awash in color, the huckleberry's reds contrast with the crustose lichen-covered rocks where barely a speck of pink granite can be found.
Photo by Carr Clifton

Left: Red maple in fall. The red maple can be distinguished from the sugar maple by the shape of its leaves. The red maple leaves have angular indentations, versus the "sugarbowl" shaped ones of the sugar maple.
Photo by Carr Clifton

Right: Morning light on Cadillac's pink granite overlooking Eagle Lake. Since the retreat of the glaciers, Acadia's landscape has changed from tundra and open woodlands to the mixed transitional forest of today.
Photo by William H. Johnson

deep, dark spruce forests. It does not harm the trees, but rather takes advantage of available space, such as the dead and dying spruce branches where sunlight no longer shines. Foliose lichens appear as mat-like leaves. Some, like rock tripe, resemble peeling brown paint. Almost every rock at Acadia is home to a variety of crustose lichens that give the pink granite the appearance of being greenish, black, or gray.

The slow colonization after glaciation by lichens as well as tundra plants began the first steps towards succession and a reforested landscape. Paleoecologists can paint a picture of these ancient landscapes through sediment analysis and by deciphering clues left behind by pollen. These microscopic grains end up in lakes and wetlands where their hard decay-resistant coats last for thousands of years. By 11,000 years ago, Maine was a mix of open woodland and tundra. As the climate began to warm, more temperate species began to move in on the more hospitable environment. Maple, oak, white pine, and birch were the prevalent trees for about 4,000 years. Hemlock, beech, and birch dominated for the next 3,000 years until the sudden and rapid decline of dominant hemlock as evidenced by a massive disappearance in the pollen record. Some populations survived, however, perhaps due to genetic resistance, and hemlock returned, along with beech and birch as the dominant forest type until about 1,500 years ago. The boreal forest began to expand south from the north, possibly due to global cooling. These new environmental conditions became hospitable to more northerly species, such as white spruce and balsam fir.

Remnants of these historic landscapes remain today as part of Acadia's transitional forest between the northern reaches of sugar maple and the southern limits of balsam fir. Acadia's geographical position, habitat variety from sea level to mountain top, and maritime climate provide a suitable environment for a diverse collection of plants representing a 2,500-mile range. Community associations of plants more common to places like Newfoundland, Labrador, and

soils, Acadia Mountain is almost desert-like with a high evaporation rate preferred by pitch pine and bear oak.

A few miles to the south of Acadia Mountain, the coastal Wonderland trail displays the association of northern and more southerly plants. Beginning with a mix of black and red spruce, representatives of both northern and southern climates, the trail opens to granite ledges dotted with pitch pines. Beneath the gnarled limbs of the pitch pine are sub-arctic plants of black crowberry and three-toothed cinquefoil, nestled next to the more southerly bayberry.

Greenland mingle with species normally found on New Jersey's southern coastal plain. Some reach their range limits at Acadia. Their study is important as they may serve as indicators of climactic change. If the climate begins to warm or cool, these species may begin to decline or increase.

Acadia Mountain's well defined forest of pitch pine and bear oak is an example of more southerly plants finding a home at Acadia. Pitch pines' short, three-needle bundles and gnarled appearance complement the shrubby nature of the bear oak. Bear oak remains small in size and has small, deeply indented leaves that are two to five inches in length. Acadia is at the northern end of its range. Although pitch pine can be found in other coastal locations northward from its predominant locations of New Jersey and Long Island, NY, the association of pitch pine with bear oak is not found again until Acadia Mountain. How did these more southerly plants end up here? One theory focuses on a time when average temperatures were warmer and the Gulf of Maine was a coastal plain connecting Newfoundland to Cape Cod. As the climate cooled, the range of these plants retreated to the south except for some patches where the area's microclimate could continue to sustain them. Acadia is one such refuge. Soil measurements also show that in comparison with other island

An example of a northern plant reaching its southern limit here is the jack pine. Although the jack pine is scattered through the park, there are two distinct stands, one on Cadillac and one at Schoodic, both registered as Maine State Critical Areas. Regeneration occurs through the opening of cones under conditions of fire or high temperature, such as on a warm sunny ledge.

Pitch pine can also be fire dependent for regeneration, but resistant to fire damage due to its thick bark. Although some succumbed to the fire of 1947, many survived. Pitch pines along the beginning ledges of the Gorham Mountain trail are over 80 years old in spite of the fire that burned this area. The dense spruce forest to the west of the trail's parking lot survived as well, but only because the fire halted before ravaging it. An excellent vantage point to see the contrast between the dark green spruce forest and the lighter green of the post-fire deciduous woods is from Gorham's ridge.

The 1947 fire, which burned 17,000 acres on Mount Desert Island, was believed to have begun near Hull's Cove. It spread rapidly, burning underground and turning into a crown fire in many areas. This type of fire is especially devastating since it burns through the tree crowns as well as the forest floor. Very few trees could survive. Fire in many forest communities is natural, playing the role of "urban renewal," the fire's scars being healed by succession.

The charred forest remains following the fire were a dismal sight, but allowed for the growth of a different forest. With no competition for sunlight, aspen and birch sprouted and grew quickly, replacing the once dominant spruce and fir forest. Although spruce prefer full sun they can tolerate shade and require it for germination. Red spruce seedlings can wait for appropriate conditions, growing in a stunted state for years. Along portions of the Park Loop Road or the Great Head trail, for example, in the shade of the fire's replacement forest of birch

show two white lines, actually a row of stomates where gas exchange takes place. Since sun is a hard commodity to come by in a spruce forest, the fir may live only 20 years or so. An easy way to tell the difference between fir and spruce is simple: "shaking hands" with a friendly fir is much easier than with a spiky spruce!

The still coolness of a mature spruce forest can be appreciated along Jordan Stream or Little Hunter's Brook. Quiet, broken only by the chatter of a red squirrel or a pileated woodpecker's call, settles between the spongy carpet of needles and the upper

and aspen, are spruce waiting to return to dominance. Very few saplings of birch or aspen can be found.

Fire is a historical part of Acadia. Soil samples indicate fire's natural frequency, prior to the arrival of Europeans, as occurring every 100 years or so. Native Americans used fire as a tool to create more diversity. These small burns probably helped to lessen the severity of large fires by reducing fuel sources. Since 1937 Acadia has had over 200 fires. Only a handful were due to natural causes. Realizing that fire is part of the Acadia ecosystem while trying to prevent another fire such as 1947, due to the proximity of local communities, is a park management concern. Instead, appropriate management techniques such as prescribed burns or mechanical (by hand!) removal of fuels is practiced.

The west side of Acadia and the western portion of the Park Loop Road beyond the ocean side contain the spruce-fir forest that characterize much of Maine. Red spruce is the dominant tree at Acadia and can be distinguished from other conifers by its half inch-long, sharp, four-sided needles carried on twigs that sport little red hairs. Red spruce forests create an environment that does not allow for much diversity, casting shade on any potential rivals. The other tree associated with spruce forests is the balsam fir. Its one-inch long flat needles are spirally arranged on the branch. The undersides

Over: The Lilliputian world of Acadia. Amidst a mosaic of rock-covered crustose lichens, reindeer moss, and blueberries find a home in the granite's cracks.
Photo by Susan Drinker

limbs of the spruce. Along these streams are other conifers that prefer moister conditions. Northern white cedar, a favorite deer browse in the winter months, is present throughout the park's wet places and alongside lake shores. It also grows on rock ledges where it seems out of place. These spots indicate an area of drainage. A tea made from the cedar's bark was given to French explorers of the New World by Native Americans. The French in turn gave it the lofty name *"arbor-vitae,"* or *"tree of life,"* since it helped them to survive scurvy.

Another moisture-loving tree, a relic of ancient Maine forests, is the hemlock. This graceful, tall tree has tiny flat needles, about one-quarter to a half inch in length and very small cones. Stands of hemlock along the Hemlock Trail at Sieur de Monts Spring and the carriage roads at both the Cobblestone and Hemlock Bridge provide welcoming shade to summer walkers and cyclists.

Two other conifers found in dryer soil are towering giants, the white pine and red pine. Historically, New England's white pines reached heights of 200 feet with a record specimen topping 240 feet.

The British Royal Navy saw perfect masts for their sailing fleets in the white pines' straight and tall trunks. The King's broad arrow slash

marked the trees that were to be cut, adding a bit more fire to the growing dislike for the crown.

The park preserves a stand of old growth white pine, as well as a stand of red spruce. The two magificent forest stands are dated to be about 200 years old.

The distinct reddish hue of the red pine's bark gave it its name. The long needles in bundles of two create a "bottle-brush" look to the tree's branches where light easily filters through. Red pine prefers gravelly soil and is often found growing on rocky ridges.

Both the white and red pine can be associated with either coniferous forests or deciduous woods. A variety of hardwood species are scattered throughout Acadia. Sugar maples, red oaks, and beech trees are examples of canopy trees, the roof of the forest. Sugar maples can be identified by their five deeply U-shaped cut leaves in comparison with the red maple's five angular indentations. Red maples can be found in moist areas and are colonizers after a fire, often suckering from roots to repopulate an area. The sugar maple, however, is intolerant of fire and usually indicates an undisturbed area. Red oaks are found throughout

the deciduous woods, their pointed, lobed leaves are among the last to leaf out in the spring. The bark's deep furrows have a light reddish tint. Although plentiful acorns fall from the red oak, their bitterness does not appeal to all wildlife. They are, however, well utilized by some insects. The acorn weevil drills a hole into the acorn and lays its eggs. The larvae feed on the inside of the acorn. Another species, the acorn moth, takes advantage of the hollowed acorn and lays her eggs inside.

While maple and oak mix with other hardwoods and conifers, Acadia's beech forests remain solitary in their make-up. Beech forests can form a monoculture if conditions are right due to their suckering tendencies. There are nearly pure stands of beech near the Bubbles. Elliptical toothed leaves and the tree's smooth gray bark are identifying characteristics. The slender cigar-like buds and small oblong beech nuts are an excellent wildlife food.

Under the canopy are understory trees, such as moosewood, or striped maple, mountain maple, shadbush, and cherry. Shrubs and herbaceous plants such as the viburnum hobblebush, the ferns, the mayflower, and the delicate starflower create two more forest

layers. Each forest level provides habitat, cover, and food for many species of plants and animals.

As both the coniferous forests and mixed woods edge out from the U-shaped valleys and up the mountain summits, they begin to change character, becoming less dense as plants adapted to open granite ledges appear. Along the mountain slopes grow one of Acadia's best known and well-loved plants, the lowbush blueberry. High-bush blueberry are found in swamps and damp thickets. June's white bell-like flowers bring mid-summer's future blueberry pies, muffins, and pancakes. Another sought after berry is the huckleberry; a plant which looks very similar to the blueberry. Inspection of the leaf's underside reveals tiny yellow resin dots that leave a sticky yellow residue on fingers. The black berries are a bit more tart and seedy, but just as delicious.

Along the mountain trails and slopes the evergreen sheep laurel sports umbels of small five-sided, cup-like pink flowers. This 2 to 3-foot shrub blooms in a beautiful display for about one month in early summer.

Moving up the mountain sides, vegetation becomes sparser. Champlain's description of Acadia's mountain tops as barren was almost correct. From a distance, many of the summits such as Cadillac, Sargent, and Champlain appear to be void of plants, but up close, the summits' low-growing plants are apparent. Despite the appearance of being above treeline, where trees will

Above left: One of Acadia's showiest summer blooming plants, the sheep laurel's pink flowers sweep across mountain slopes such as Beech Mountain.
Photo by William H. Johnson

Above: Peeking through the reindeer moss, one of the forest floor's gems: the starflower.
Photo by Glenn Van Nimwegen

Left: Lupines seem to be a natural part of Acadia even though they are not native to the area. Twenty five percent of all plants in Acadia are non-native.
Photo by Tom Till

no longer grow, these mountains are not high enough for that distinction. The lack of soil, coupled with the full force of wind and the elements, do however create difficult living conditions that mimic treeline conditions.

Plants best suited for life here are those that can hunker down taking advantage of granite crevices. Species such as the sub-arctic

three-toothed cinquefoil thrive in these dry, rocky cracks. Although these plants withstand extreme environmental stresses, they are fragile and can fall victim to trampling. Visitors are urged to remain on marked trails.

Plant species commonly growing at lower elevations may be represented on these summits by a few individuals. They grow in what resemble miniature landscapes of "bonsai" grouped in small granite depressions where they take advantage of the collected moisture and soil.

Their stunted growth is due to high winds, little soil, and the stress of life on exposed mountain summits caked in winter ice.

From mountain summits to the coastline, coastal plants have their own set of stresses. At times plants bathe in moist sea air, other times they are whipped by strong winds. Fresh water can be scarce while salt spray may be in abundance. Coastline soil mostly consists of eroding granite particles found in pockets along the rocks. These thin acidic soils, along with the climate conditions, dictate which plants will take hold. Examples of these hardy plants are found along Acadia's rocky shores.

White spruce, a large tree with a somewhat whitish hue to its green needles, requires cool to cold conditions for optimal growth. Widely distributed to the north of Acadia and throughout Canada, it can be found hugging the Maine coastline due to cooler summer temperatures. Bayberry withstands the drying winds due to its waxy cuticle-covered leaves which help to conserve moisture. This shrub's roots take nitrogen from the atmosphere to add to the soil. Carpeting the upper rocks is the arctic species black crowberry, a dark green spiky plant that bears little pinkish flowers which become red berries. Mingling among these plants is the rugosa rose, a plant that easily defines a Maine coast

Above left: Carpeting sunny areas on woodland floors is the bunchberry, a member of the dogwood family. Its flowers consist of four showy white bracts that surround the small inconspicuous flowers. These will bear red berries in the fall.
Photo by Glenn Van Nimwegen

Above right: The heavy rose perfume of rugosa rose hangs in Acadia's moist summer sea air. Brought to this country to help control erosion, it is now common along the northeastern coast.
Photo by Glenn Van Nimwegen

Right: Cinnamon ferns and blue flag iris prefer moist places. Many species of ferns inhabit rocky ledges, meadows, forests, and swamps in Acadia.
Photo by William H. Johnson

memory with it's overwhelming perfume. Not native to the United States, they were brought from Japan centuries ago to the East Coast to help control erosion along the shoreline.

Acadia's wetlands include bogs, marshes, lakes, ponds, and

streams. They provide vital habitats and needed breeding grounds for many species and add their unique touch to the park's personality. The breathtaking view of the Bubbles across Jordan Pond, the "high country" feel of Bubble Pond, the open shrubby shore at Witch Hole Pond, or the refreshing surprise of a mountain pool such as the Bowl atop the Beehive, are an integral part of the Acadia experience. Spring waterfalls racing down mountain sides, the roaring stream of Jordan Pond after an intense rain, and the symphony of birds along a marsh all add their own flavor.

Acadia's 22 lakes and ponds range in size from a few acres to almost 900 and are home to 24 species of fish, including the brook trout, the lake trout, the landlocked salmon, and the smallmouth bass. Many fish species are stocked by the State of Maine. Waterfowl such as the wood duck, the mallard, and the black duck, along with other birds can be spotted. Many ponds and

lakes fall entirely within Acadia's borders while some are shared with surrounding communities. Acadia's water resources are not immune to outside threats. Impacts include development adjacent to parkland, sewage disposal, and atmospheric deposition. Selected lakes are monitored by park staff for water quality. In general, they are considered healthy, but continued monitoring is critical for their conservation.

Succession, the natural replacement of one community with another, is a part of lake and pond ecosystems, just as it was following glacial ice and the fire of 1947. The Tarn, a shallow lake between Dorr Mountain and Huguenot Head is in the midst of this natural process. The accumulation of sediment, dead microscopic plankton, and decaying plants add muck to the Tarn's shallow bottom allowing surface floating plants, like waterlilies and duckweeds, to root. These aquatic plants provide new habitats for dragonflies, mayflies, frogs, and beetles. Emergent aquatics such as cattails, sedges, bulrushes, and pickerelweed now grow, adding a new habitat for snails, red-winged black birds, muskrats, grackles, and ducks. This is the current stage of the Tarn. Slowly the lack of oxygen and the constant decay of plants may build up enough soil for the lake to change into a marsh. Grasses and herbaceous plants such as meadowsweet, golden rod, and wild rose will join, as well as moisture loving shrubs such as winterberry and deciduous alders. Snowshoe hare, field mice, yellow warblers, eastern king birds, and phoebes will arrive once the sun-loving wetland plants become part of the new system. Great Meadow, behind Sieur de Monts Spring and north of the Tarn, is an example of the possible direction the Tarn's succession is headed.

Bogs are part of Acadia's freshwater wetlands. Year after year, the accumulation of decomposed vegetation, in particular sphagnum moss, creates peat, the bog's foundation. The coffee-colored water is due to the high levels of tannic acid released from this slow decay. There are numerous boggy areas throughout the park, which in addition to the unusual carnivorous pitcher plant and sundew, house some rare plant species.

For visitors unable to visit all of Acadia's landscape diversity, the Wild Gardens of Acadia at Sieur de Monts Spring provides an outstanding opportunity to discover many of the park's habitats and their associated plants.

Above: White birch, along with quaking aspen and big tooth aspen, colonized the void left after the 1947 fire. The understory finds red spruce waiting their chance to dominate again.
Below: Dorr Mountain carpeted in the golden colors of a fall early morning freeze. The forest slowly succumbs to the lack of soil and harsher conditions of Acadia's upper mountain slopes and summits.
Photos by Glenn Van Nimwegen

Right: Fall forest in an explosion of bright colors. The spectacular change of color begins slowly in early September, peaking the first two weeks of October. Shorter days and cooler temperatures trigger trees to stop production of chlorophyll. As the green chlorophyll dies, the pigments present in the leaves appear more brilliant. Aspens, birch, and beech are draped in yellow, red maples in scarlet, sugar maples in a mix of yellow, orange, and brilliant reds.
Photo by Jeff Foott

THE COAST

A favorite site along the ocean, Thunder Hole draws many visitors, especially during coastal storms. Thunder Hole booms when air, which had been trapped by waves entering a narrow rock chamber, is released in a resounding burst. The best time to catch Thunder Hole thundering, rather than sloshing, is around mid-tide rising.
Photo by Glenn Van Nimwegen

Acadia National Park sits on the edge of one of the world's most biologically active and productive areas, the Gulf of Maine. Stretching from the outstretched arm of Cape Cod to the southern end of Nova Scotia, this semi-enclosed body of water's eastern underwater boundary is 200 miles offshore at Georges Bank. A very young body of water, the Gulf's most recent bottom topography was born directly of glacial action. Ice and meltwater gouged and deepened the hills, valleys, river bottoms, and plains present from an earlier time. Today the Gulf comprises a variety of habitats from open sea to tidal marshes. Estuaries, tidal wetlands, rocky shores, and islands contain hundreds of bird species, more than 100 types of fish, 1,600 bottom dwellers, and 26 species of marine mammals. Acadia National Park and its surrounding waters is home to a variety of these inhabitants.

Historically, mariners titled this comparatively shallow basin next to the Atlantic a "sea next to a sea." A series of shallow banks, remnants of glaciation, keep the Gulf separate. These shelves slope gently toward the west, but drop steeply on the Atlantic side. The 22-mile wide Northeast Channel between the two largest banks, Georges (to the south) and Browns (to the north), provides an inlet to siphon water from the Atlantic. The average depth of the productive fishing grounds of Georges Bank are 192 feet deep, although some areas are only 9 feet deep.

Seven major rivers, large tidal fluctuations, and winds drive the Gulf's water circulation in a counter-clockwise pattern. Other factors influencing this movement include the

Preceding pages: Rolling Island off of Schoodic, one of the 5,000 or so islands dotting the coast of Maine.
Photo by Willard Clay

Left: Along the Park Loop Road looking east to the Beehive and Champlain Mountain. Diversity reigns along Acadia's Gulf of Maine shore with every rock, crack, and crevice between high and low tide housing an intertidal occupant. Here barnacles populate shore rocks.
Photo by David Muench

Right: Otter Cliffs. "Pull up a granite slab and sit awhile" the locals will tell you. It's one of the best ways to discover Acadia's peace.
Photo by Glenn Van Nimwegen

Labrador current wrapping around Nova Scotia and the deflection of the river outflows to the right by Earth's rotation. These rivers are also major contributors to the productivity of the Gulf. Tumbling from the land's mountains and plateaus, the yearly influx of 250 billion gallons of fresh water carries minerals, snow melt, and decaying plant particles. This organic "soup" mixes with the saltwater of the Gulf, while wave and tidal action stir the waters so nutrients are moved from the deep waters to the Gulf's upper layers. This rich mix slowly circles the Gulf every three months, providing a nutrient base to support the intricate food webs of plankton, invertebrates, fish, marine mammals, and birds. In addition, the Gulf's cold waters support large amounts of biological activity since cold water holds more oxygen.

Protection of the Gulf ecosystem is important as over-development of coastal areas and toxic run-offs from industry and agriculture could adversely affect Gulf habitats and their associated wildlife populations. Of Maine's 2,500 miles of coastline, only 150 are preserved in the public domain. Twenty five percent are in Acadia National Park and include rocky cliffs and tidepools; sand, boulder, and cobble beaches; mud flats and tidal marshes; plus off-shore islands. These environments are greatly affected by the tides.

Tides are caused primarily by the gravitational pull of the moon, and to some extent, of the sun. The moon's orbital position dictates high or low tides. As the earth completes its daily 24 hour rotation, each point on the planet will have traveled through the moon's gravitational pull. High tide is the result of that temporary alignment. On the opposite side of the earth, away from the moon, a high tide is occurring due to centrifugal force. A low tide occurs in between the high tide bulges. Tides occur 50 minutes later each day because the moon takes about 50 minutes longer to orbit the earth than the earth's 24 hour rotation.

When the moon is new or full and in line with the sun, the tides are greater. These "spring" tides occur because the gravitational pull is increased by the sun's alignment with the moon. When the moon is at an angle to the sun, the two gravitational pulls partially cancel each other out and "neap" tides occur.

Because many factors affect the tides, different global locations may experience tides only twice a day, or tide intervals of various times or heights. Acadia has semidiurnal tides, with highs and lows happening about twice a day. The elliptical orbit of the moon, the equinox and solstice, and the shape and depth of the ocean floor all contribute to the tidal equation. The depth of the Gulf of Maine partially explains the large tidal height of the region, ranging from 6 feet along Cape Cod to 50 feet in the Bay of Fundy. As tidal water from the deep Atlantic traverses the shallow Gulf its contact with the irregular coastline results in large tides.

Acadia's tidal range is between 8 and 12 feet. These large tidal variations have influenced varied adaptations within the plants and animals living in a world both submerged by seawater and exposed to air. On the rocky shores, every crack, crevice, and depression creates a different habitat for an incredible collection of

creatures. These tidepool "aquariums" are fascinating places.

The lowest point of the lowest tide is a place where it will always be wet, but between that place and the highest of the high tides are places that will, at one time or another, either occasionally or often, be exposed without the cover of sea water. Conditions change as do the corresponding organisms within a few feet, sometimes a few inches. Who lives where is determined by this difference in submergence versus exposure. Due to this, different "zones" can be distinguished by the indicator plant or animal species that is associated with that area.

The splash zone never sees the highest tides, it only receives the splash of their waves; enough for certain organisms to survive. This mix of splash and rainwater results in fluctuations of salinity levels. The orange-yellow Xanthoria lichen lives in this zone. It receives all it needs to survive from rainfall and the spray of ocean waves.

The highest of high tides reaches the black zone, dominated by dark blue-green algae. Half of each month they will never be submerged. These one-celled algae are encased in a gelatinous sheath, protecting them from drying when exposed to the atmosphere. Blue-green algae supply massive amounts of oxygen and may be responsible for the earth's early oxygen atmosphere. Fossil evidence dates their presence to 2 billion years.

The whitish band below the black zone is very distinctive. This domain belongs to the barnacle, their volcano-like white shells crammed side by side. They remain dry about 70% of the time. Perhaps one of the most enjoyable tidepool creatures to watch,

the barnacle, is a relative of crabs and lobsters. Before settling on a rock, the free-swimming larva resembles a minute clam. Within a few moments of becoming rockbound, the barnacle cements its head in place and transforms calcium carbonate secretions into a six-section house with a four piece trap door. There it will live for 3 to 5 years. During the rush of high tide, the barnacle's feathery legs emerge from the trap door to gather food, mostly plankton, from the waters.

Bands of olive-green seaweed strands dominate the mid-tide zone, a place that falls between the extremes of the low and high neap tide. These forests of rockweeds rise and fall with the tide. They are characterized by air bladders that help keep the plants afloat when the tide comes in. Bladder wrack has flattened ribs with air bladders and receptacles for sexual reproduction at its tips. Knotted wrack bladders are at intervals along its thin rope-like blades. These two species account for most of the exposed seaweed in the intertidal zone and provide a haven for small animals to hide amongst. Rockweeds are fairly tolerant of exposure but need to be submerged for at least one hour during each high tide. Their back and forth swaying helps

to break the impact of the crashing surf. The pressure of big waves can often run as high as one ton per square foot.

The fourth zone, represented by the red algae irish moss, is not as obvious as the other three. Irish moss' low growing, frilly tufts show an iridescent purple on their blade tips when sunlight reflects off them. Irish moss contains carrageenan, a stabilizer which, when extracted, is used in many processed foods such as salad dressing and ice cream.

The kelp zone is always covered by water, except during one of the four yearly extreme spring tides. Kelps have very few adaptations to protect them from exposure to the atmosphere. There are a variety of these large brown seaweeds which can grow up to 20 feet along the Maine coast. Some kelps have an unusual appearance, such as buckshot or sea colander, which has hundreds of holes throughout its blades, an adaptation resulting in less resistance to the waves.

The rocky coastline is the dominant feature of the Maine coast. Geologically speaking, very few years have passed to allow for the erosion of these dominating granite cliffs and rocky ledges. Acadia's coast is in its infancy and its lack of beaches is indicative of this.

Left: Newport Cove looking along the shore to Great Head. Acadia's rockbound coast is still in its infancy, awaiting eons of erosion to consistently reshape it. **Photo by James Randklev**

Below: Bass Harbor Marsh in early fall. Salt marshes are some of the most productive habitats, harboring a vast variety of life from tidal creatures to shorebirds

and visiting mammals. **Photo by John Shaw**

Above: Sand Beach's development is due in part to its sheltered location in Newport Cove. A handful of sand blends an amazing mix of colors, mostly composed from the shells of intertidal creatures. **Photo by Willard Clay**

A World Between Tides

High tides covering the intertidal area cloak a rich variety of life, only to reveal it six hours later as the tide recedes. A variety of habitats between the tides, from the splash zone to the

kelp zone, are home to many specially adapted plants and animals including more than 100 different marine invertebrates.

Three different periwinkles can be found along the shore, each at different levels. Rough periwinkles, the smallest of the three, dwell at the edge of the high tide line, spending little time submerged. The common periwinkle, found in the rockweed zone, has a brownish shell with six to seven whorls to its point. The smooth periwinkle is usually found a little lower; its shell appears to be more flattened at the top than the common periwinkle. Periwinkles are gastropods who feed by scraping algae with their sandpaper like tongue, called a radula. To withstand low tides and to prevent drying out, the snail closes its operculum, a trap door keeping moisture within the shell.

Dog whelks are carnivorous snails often found in the middle to lower zones. The dog whelk's pointed shell comes in a variety of colors such as orange, brown, yellow, and striped. Its drill-like radula bores holes into mussels and barnacles, secreting an acid to dissolve the shell. A small amount of muscle relaxant is then excreted, causing the shelled animal to liquefy. Egg cases of the dog whelk resemble colonies of small grains of rice.

The limpet, another gastropod like the periwinkle and dog whelk, is a little hat-like snail, gray or brown in color. The limpet feeds on algae, scraping it from the rocks with its radula. Limpets hold on to rocks with a great deal of force and should not be disturbed.

Sea stars, commonly called starfish, are also found. These creatures are members of the echinoderm family characterized by five-part radial symmetry and spiny skin. Relatives include the sea urchins and sea cucumbers. Sea stars are covered with tiny pinchers, called pedicillarea, that remove plants or animals attempting to stick on their bodies. Suction cup-like tube feet are the sea star's way of holding on to rocks. Eyespots for noting differences in light intensity are found on the ends of the sea star's arms, while its mouth is centrally located underneath.

The sea cucumber inhabits the tidepools as well. An odd creature resembling a cucumber, it exhibits the same radial symmetry of other echinoderms with five rows of tube feet down its sides. The sea cucumber's mouth has tentacle-like structures around it for bringing in food. When threatened, this creature may eject portions of its internal organs in hopes of satisfying the predator. The sea cucumber then regenerates its lost organs.

Sea urchins live on the floors of deeper tidepools, but are often found broken on the shoreline rocks, dropped by gulls attempting to crush them. Echinoderms too, they resemble small green pincushions. Although they do not appear to have radial symmetry, closer inspection reveals five teeth in the mouth (called Aristotle's Lantern) and five rows of tube feet, especially evident on the inside of a discarded shell. Sea urchins are grazers, scraping algae from the rocks with their teeth.

Another animal present in Acadia's tidepools is the sea anemone. Animals, not plants, the anemones are related to the jellyfish. They consist of a pedal disc for attachment to rocks and a thick stalk topped with hundreds of frilly tentacles. These tentacles contain specialized cells called nematocysts, which they use to capture their prey.

Crabs are present too, especially hiding among the rockweed. The green crabs, about 1 to 3 inches across, are small, active, and feisty little biters who will defend themselves when provoked. The hermit crab, always a delight to children, can be found hiding in discarded periwinkle shells. Without a hard outer shell, or exoskeleton of their own, they have to borrow one to protect their soft body and survive. The rock crabs are also common. Reddish-brown to yellowish, they can grow to over five inches and have nine well developed spikes or

"teeth" along the margins of their shell.

The seaweeds along the shore (see text) are vital to the entire tidepool ecosystem. All seaweeds are algaes. In general, they consist of a holdfast for gripping, a stem-like stipe, and a blade which absorbs nutrients and photosynthesizes. The shapes of seaweeds, from the stringy rockweeds to the clinging algaes like irish moss, are all adapted to withstand the stress and pressure of pounding waves.

Above left: Barnacles and dog whelks. Dog whelks, predators of the intertidal zone, come in a variety of colors from orange to brown to striped.
Photo by John Netherton

Above: Example of zonation. The bands of different colors define the dominant plants and animals of the intertidal zone, each adapted to specific tide levels and exposure to the elements.
Photo by Glenn Van Nimwegen

Left: Man O'War Brook, Somes Sound. Blue mussels are present throughout Acadia's coastline. Usually living in large colonies, they inhabit the middle range of the intertidal zone.
Photo by Michael Melford

When beaches exist, they usually consist of gravel, pebble, cobblestone, or boulders, and their development is dependent on sediment accretion and erosion. Cobble and boulder beaches can be found in pockets where the rocky cliffs have eroded away. Although these cliffs may look solid in the wake of a thundering ocean, they break apart bit by bit. Chunks of rock fall from fractures to join others being tossed and rounded in the pounding surf, eventually to be deposited in pocket coves among the cliffs.

Near Gorham Mountain, Monument Cove's slope and harsh wave action resulted in a boulder beach. The solitary granite monument is testimony to the effects of the ocean eating away at the weaker rock. Small sediments, even cobbles, are rarely deposited here, because the high surf energy simply carries them away.

Cobble beaches are created from fragmented rock and off-shore glacial till rounded and smoothed by tumbling waves, and where beach slope is no more than 20 %. Cobbles are 2 ½ to 8 ½ inches in diameter. Smaller, and they are classified as gravel or pebbles. Larger and they are boulders. The area around Seawall has numerous cobble beaches and a natural "seawall," formed from the tossing of rocks during storms. Unfortunately, this natural seawall has grown smaller, not by the ocean, but by the actions of park visitors unaware of the park's "no collecting" policy.

Sand beaches are rare along the Maine coast. Acadia's Sand Beach is located in Newport Cove, a wide, flat, U-shaped cove that is abutted by steep cliffs and the long arm of the Great Head peninsula. Great Head and the large ledge at the mouth of the cove, Old Soaker, channel calmer waters with their sediment load into the cove. As the waves lose energy, heavier particles, such as gravel and cobbles, drop to the sea floor. The smallest particles come to rest on the beach.

A handful of Sand Beach sand is a kaleidoscope of color. The pink, white, and gray grains indicate their connection at one time to the rocky cliffs. The blue, green, white, and yellow chips once belonged to the shells of intertidal creatures such as barnacles, mussels, and sea urchins. Seventy percent of Sand Beach's sand is composed of the remains of these animals. The source of these shell fragments are believed to be local, right from the beach's rock-bound sides. Behind Sand Beach is another product of accretion: sand dunes. The constant addition of sand grains, one by one, shaped by the wind into sheets, drives dune development. The dominant American beach grass, stabilizes the sand. The dunes, in addition to the unique nature of the sand, have made Sand Beach a National Natural Landmark and a Maine State Critical Area.

The same factors that hinder the development of beaches make extensive tidal marshes, such as those to the south of Cape Cod, rare. However, in sheltered areas where the slope of the land is slight and the rocky coast has eroded away, sediment build-up has allowed for the development of these biologically rich habitats.

Above: Storms in the Gulf of Maine bring dangerous but spectacular surf along Acadia's rocky shoreline. Waves, crashing on the rocks with great force, give birth to sea water geysers sometimes reaching 80 feet in the air.
Photo by Glenn Van Nimwegen

Below: Thick ice cakes the salt marsh and tidal areas around Thompson Island. Winters are milder now than in the 1920's when ice often froze the inland waterways and harbors.
Photo by William H. Johnson

The birth of a marsh has its beginnings in mud. Mud's fine particles remain suspended in water until very calm waters, such as those in quiet coves and harbors, allow them to settle. One quiet cove is Ship Harbor, on Acadia's west side, where a mix of slow waters and minimal slope allows fine sediments to settle, creating a mud flat.

Mud creates a habitat that only specifically adapted animals can survive in. By their very nature, mud particles cling together, leaving little room for oxygen to get through. The characteristic rotten egg smell of a mudflat indicates oxygen's rapid decrease.

submerged under saltwater. Eelgrass filters salt from the water using salt glands that remove the sodium and chlorine ions.

At Ship Harbor dark patches of eelgrass beds are visible under the water. Eelgrass stabilizes the substrate and catches detritus for animals to feed on. The blades produce a surface for small animals to clutch on to while the extensive tangled mats provide shelter for many organisms, especially larval stages of invertebrates, shellfish, and some fish. This in turn attracts seabirds such as herons, egrets, and gulls that pick and pluck at these beds.

Life without oxygen is impossible for almost all organisms, yet many creatures inhabit the mud. Creatures such as the amphitrite, a tube building worm who forms a u-shaped tube from sticky mud particles; the clamworm, which can grow up to three feet long; and the bloodworm, all thrive in this environment.

Like the mud-dwelling worms, the burrowing soft-shelled clam needs a way to get oxygen. The clam uses a fleshy tube called a siphon, that in addition to oxygen, brings in water and food while it extrudes waste. The long siphon, which can stretch up to three times the clam's length, retracts as the clam senses pressure on the mud; hence possible predation. This retraction causes a little squirt of water, actually revealing the clam's location.

The mud's surface is home to wayward mussels and barnacles that manage to get a foothold on rocks of all sizes, as well as to the green crab. Approximately two inches in length, the green crab is not indigenous to this country. It arrived via ships from the British Isles and then spread north from the Cape Cod area in the 19th century. Today, they are one of the most common crabs found in the Northeast.

In the calm waters of a mudflat, eelgrass grows, playing a major role in the productivity of marshes and mudflat areas. It is one of the few true marine plants with flowers, seeds, and roots constantly

Eelgrass beds can help to create tidal marshes. As more detritus and mud particles are trapped, the substrate begins to grow inch by inch, paving the way for salt marsh colonizers.

Salt marshes are highly productive areas creating tons of biomass per acre each year. They nourish coastal seas by dispensing organic materials needed for the life cycles of many marine plants, shellfish, and other marine invertebrates while filtering out substances that could be harmful. Grasses spring with insects, dragonflies dart overhead, ducks paddle through tidal creeks, while red-winged blackbirds and swallows dive for insects. Long-legged shorebirds patiently wait for fish to swim by. Intertidal creatures such as mussels and periwinkles inhabit the surface of the muddy bottom, while clams and worms burrow beneath. Along the marsh edges where forests of birch and spruce begin, deer graze. Even red fox and raccoons wander through the marsh in search of a green crab meal.

Only a few plants living in both a terrestrial and aquatic world are capable of withstanding partial daily submergence by salt water. Plants specially adapted to the saline conditions establish themselves according to the tide's reach, the primary factor dictating which salt marsh plants grow where. Once the first colonizers set root, they assist in the process of creating a salt marsh by trapping sediment and slowing down wave action so particles can be deposited. Cordgrass, a coarse thick grass, helps stabilize the marsh. It grows so densely that few other plants can squeeze in. Cordgrass withstands the greatest amount of saltwater, requiring regular flooding. Scattered among the cordgrass is *salicornia*, a jointed, stubby succulent that is an edible treat. Its variety of common names such as chickentoe, pickleweed, saltwort, and glasswort are all aptly descriptive.

Along the upper edges of the tidal areas, salt hay grows. Much finer and shorter than cordgrass, its cowlicked clumps swirl in

marsh hay and used large marshes for cattle grazing. Today however, pressures on salt marshes are much greater than the limited historical use. Many have been dredged to provide harbors and waterways for boats or filled to create land. Unfortunately, removal of salt marshes disrupts the important role they play as a nursery for the larval stage of hundreds of marine organisms, including 70 % of all commercial fish and shellfish later harvested. Prime habitat for nesting waterfowl is lost and the marsh's ability to filter contaminants and to slow shore erosion is destroyed.

matted half-circles. Salt hay is almost entirely removed from tidal influence except for spring tides, which must cover it at some time. Without this bi-monthly submergence, certain terrestrial plants would out-compete the salt hay. At the very upper limit of the tidal area grows black grass, a thin rush with a deep-green, blackish hue. Another salt marsh plant is sea lavender. Found at the tide's edge, it is able to withstand the salt spray.

How do these plants handle saltwater? Like eel-grass, they have special adaptations to bring freshwater through their roots while excreting out salt. Osmosis, the process of bringing water into the cells, requires water to move from areas of higher concentration to those of less in a solution. By collecting large quantities of salt within their roots, the plants create an imbalance allowing water molecules to enter the plant's cells. This "almost fresh" water can than be utilized. The remaining salt is excreted through the salt glands, appearing on the grass blades as salt, or salty tasting droplets. Oxygen uptake is another tricky matter since marsh mud holds little. Through very well-developed air tubes in the blades, salt marsh plants efficiently use the available oxygen.

Historically, Native Americans used marshes in New England for fertilizer and for trapping small fish. Waterfowl eggs and clams were gathered, as well as edible plants. Colonists harvested salt

Above: Morning mist behind Sand Beach. Looming in the background beyond the dunes is the Beehive. The fragile dunes are stabilized by stands of American beach grass. Feet should refrain from walking on them!
Photo by Susan G. Drinker

Bass Harbor, on Acadia's west side, is a tidal marsh with a spectacular backdrop of mountains. It has its own share of threats. The marsh is not completely within the park boundary and has a freshwater tributary whose source is close to a landfill.

At times it is hard to remember that Acadia is an island, considering all that it harbors. The approximately 5,000 islands off the Maine coast range in size from small rock outcroppings, pancake size islands, to the large Mount Desert Island and Swans Island. Many are hilltop remnants, the hills beneath and their valleys drowned in sea water. Diversity varies on these islands, dependent on size, previous human activity (logging, grazing, etc.), distance from mainland, soil conditions, and habitat suitability. Some are barren, with only a few sparse grasses, while others are covered with dense forests.

Acadia preserves numerous smaller islands, as well as the larger Isle au Haut, and holds title to conservation easements of many more. One of the most spectacular views of Mount Desert Island is part of the lure of Acadia's Baker Island. From its shore,

Acadia's mountain summits roll across the horizon. Baker Island is a very special place with open meadows, dense forests, and spectacular granite block storm beach; one of the best examples found along the Maine coast.

In Frenchman Bay, the stepping-stone Porcupine Islands belong to Acadia and the Nature Conservancy (Long Porcupine). Bald Porcupine Island's spruce-topped cliffs resemble a receding hairline. Despite the balding appearance, it probably received its name from the bald eagles which nest here. Many Maine islands are important habitat for this species, as well as for osprey.

A Native American legend explains how these "porcupine" islands appeared in the middle of Frenchman Bay. As a mythical figure climbed the highest island mountain, he was persistently pestered by a group of four porcupines. By the time he reached the summit, his patience had worn thin and he booted each one down to the bay beneath where they remain today as islands. However, geologic forces and glacial carving, rather than an agitated being, are responsible for their shape and overall topography (see Geology).

Historically, islands were quickly settled, their closeness to fishing grounds and transportation coveted. Nesting seabirds have always considered them prime real estate as well. Unfortunately for many seabirds, human and bird interests clashed during the 1800's. Egg collecting on the islands was quite common. Evidence of this is found on coastal maps by the presence of numerous "egg rocks," including one in Frenchman Bay. To assure a fresh batch of eggs, collectors would smash the first round of eggs, then collect the next eggs that were laid. After a century of egg collection, along with hunting for feathers and meat, some seabird species, such as the great auk, became extinct. Other species almost had their populations decimated. Seabird protection at the turn of the century was one of the first conservation acts in this country. A direct result of these efforts was the creation of the Audubon Society and the rebound of seabird populations. Eiders, harlequin ducks, terns, puffins, and guillemots all have nesting territory on Maine islands. Some populations, such as the herring gull, have increased in great numbers.

Although not all of the 5,000 islands off the coast are in public protection, many are held as conservation easements. Private citizens who desire to see these islands remain protected choose to give up certain rights to the land, such as lumbering and development. These restrictions remain even when ownership changes hands. Access, unless stated by the landowner, is not open to the public. The easement in turn is granted to a conservation agency who holds it. Acadia holds over one hundred easements, protecting the land in its natural state for perpetuity.

Above: There are more than 2,500 miles of coastline found in Maine, but only 150 miles are protected. Twenty-five percent of these are protected within Acadia National Park.
Photo by John Netherton
Below: Light piercing through the clouds over Somes Sound. Somesville was named

after Abraham Somes, the first white settler who, after arriving from Gloucester, Massachusetts in 1759, established a permanent residency on the island. This first settlement, growing to a small town by 1770, took advantage of the protective coastal setting at the end of Somes Sound.
Photo by Glenn Van Nimwegen

THE LOBSTER

A trip to the Maine coast would be incomplete for most Acadia visitors without lobster. An integral part of Maine's economy, lobsters adorn everything from T-shirts to, at one time, the state's license plate.

Invertebrates, lobsters are equipped with a hard exoskeleton, four pairs of "walking legs" and a pair of strong asymmetrical claws used for different purposes. The larger one, the crusher claw, is usually more rounded and is used for crushing and cracking objects such as the shells of prey. The smaller one, the pincher claw, is more slender and sharper and is used for cutting and tearing the food apart.

Lobsters shed their exoskeleton with each increase in size. They can grow to 4 feet, weigh as much as 45 pounds, and may live up to 100 years. Summer lobsters often have soft-shells, the result of this molting.

Lobsters are scavengers. Primarily nocturnal, they roam the sea floor in search of crabs, mussels, worms, sea urchins, and other sea floor invertebrates. Lobstermen bait their traps with dead fish to take advantage of their scavenging nature. The trap is designed to allow lobsters to enter but not escape.

Responding to sea water temperature changes, lobsters migrate between both shallow waters and deep off-shore areas up to 2,000 feet deep. The sea floor in the Maine mid-coast area is largely composed of boulders and crevices, the preferred shelter of lobsters. Correspondingly so, lobster harvests are larger in this region. This rocky sea floor provides good cover, assuring a greater survival rate for young lobsters.

Maine produces half the lobsters sold in the United States as well as one quarter of the world's supply. The majority of lobsters are landed between July and November. The average annual catch in recent years has ranged between 20 and 30 million pounds. Between 1880 and 1910, the catch ranged between 10 and 20 million pounds. It would seem that the variance between these two numbers would indicate a recent increase in lobster landings. What is not shown, however, is the effort involved in the catch which has sustained a four-fold increase since the turn of the century with far more traps and lobstermen using modern techniques. These figures thus show a smaller ratio of lobsters per-fisherman caught.

Indeed lobsters used to be so plentiful they could be plucked from tidepools. Their common use as a fertilizer may surprise people who just paid $18.95 for a lobster

Above: Due to numerous conservation measures, such as size limits and releasing egg-bearing females, the Maine lobster population is stronger today than a few years ago.
Photo by Michele Stapleton

Right: Lobstering is a tough business. Weather conditions are not always ideal and traps can be lost in storms and washed ashore. Unlike this older wooden trap, most lobstermen today use metal traps that withstand the elements and time much better.
Photo by Willard Clay

dinner. Regarded as "trash" food, servants considered themselves fortunate if they didn't have to eat lobster more than twice a week!

Maine's conservation laws regarding lobster catches are to protect the stability of the fishery. Minimum catch size, as measured from the head to the start of the tail, has increased in the last few years; currently it is around three and a quarter inches. Maximum size limit for capture is five inches. No more than 100 lobsters can be caught a day and only 500 are allowed per multi-day lobstering trip. If a female bearing eggs is caught, she must be thrown back, but not until a V-shaped notch is cut in her tail. This marking assures her she will never be kept if caught, but will always be released to continue to reproduce. Permits and licenses are required, as is a maximum trap size limit.

The average number of traps per boat has risen since the late 1960's from 250 to close to 600. Almost all lobster traps in use today are wire, no longer the scenic wooden ones of postcards. Although wire traps withstand the elements better, a potential drawback occurs when traps break from their lines. Wooden traps will eventually disintegrate, but wire ones continue to snare animals indefinitely. To prevent this ghost trapping, wire traps are required to have an escape panel that breaks down over time.

The brightly colored lobster buoys with different patterns and colors distinguish individual lobstermen's traps. They must display a sample buoy on their lobster boat and only collect traps with the corresponding buoy. There are no set territories for lobstermen to fish. There may be unspoken ones however!

Lobstering is difficult work. It is one of the last industries shaped by the labor of independent individuals. Watching a lobsterman in action is to see a whirlwind of motion. Traps are hauled up, opened, and the contents examined. Lobsters are quickly measured, and if of legal size, their waving claws are clamped with thick rubber bands. Illegal-sized lobsters and egg bearing females are tossed back, along with sea urchins, sea stars, and other creatures that have found their way in. The traps are baited again and thrown overboard. All of this happens in a matter of short minutes, and the lobsterman heads to the next trap. The end result? That delicious part of any Maine memory - a lobster dinner.

WILDLIFE

Scattered throughout Acadia's varied habitats are 40 species of terrestrial mammals, 11 species of amphibians, 7 species of reptiles, and 273 different species of observed birds. The number of invertebrates easily exceeds the total above. Discovering Acadia's wildlife is not difficult, although it requires patience, careful observation and an awareness of where and when animals are active. Many are nocturnal, or active in the hours around dawn and dusk. Looking for wildlife also requires searching for small clues. The square-chiseled tree holes from the pileated woodpecker, the beaver-chewed stumps, the call of the loon, or the evening trill of the hermit thrush are often as rewarding as sighting the actual animal. When seeking the wild in Acadia, binoculars and field guides are helpful tools to accompany quiet feet and still voices. To avoid disturbing wildlife, dogs must be leashed.

In Acadia's coniferous forests perhaps the most common creature is the red squirrel, which scurries from tree to tree. Its *rat-a-tat-tat* scolding breaks the silence of these dark forests. The aftermath of a red squirrel's meal of red spruce cones litters rocks, decaying logs, and the forest floor. Northern flying squirrels are the nocturnal counterpart to the red squirrel, their large eyes well adapted for their nighttime forays. The large skin flaps along their bodies give the illusion of flight as they leap from tree to tree.

The park's mixed and deciduous woods offer much more habitat variety and food. Eastern chipmunks are the obvious rodents of this forest, but just as common, although unseen, are smaller rodents such as the masked shrew. The white-tailed deer roam freely, gathering their

The national symbol, the bald eagle flies high over Acadia's surrounding waters, in search of fish and seabirds. Bald eagles' slow recovery from the edge of extinction resulted in their status being changed from endangered to threatened on July 4, 1995. On July 2, 1999 President Clinton announced the removal of the bald eagle from the list by July 2000. Today, there are more than 5,800 breeding pairs throughout the nation. At Acadia and in Maine, their rebound has not been as strong. Studies indicate persistent pollutants in Maine soils may be to blame.
Photo by Bill Silliker Jr.

Preceding pages: Early morning sun rays touch Cadillac's granite slopes, while Bar Harbor, Frenchman Bay, and the Porcupine Islands lie at the mountain's base. On clear days, you can faintly see the summit of Mt. Kathadin, two hours to the north.
Photo by Jeff Gnass

Left: White-tailed deer buck. Although white-tailed deer populations have skyrocketed in other parts of the country, Acadia's population remains low. Studies indicate the presence of coyote on the island may be a factor.
Photo by Len Rue Jr.

Right: The eastern coyote is a relative newcomer to Acadia National Park. Sometime in the early 1980's coyotes crossed to the island, bringing their haunting howls to Acadia.
Photo by Len Rue Jr.

favorite browse of cedar, pine, maple, and birch in addition to other delicacies like acorns and clover. Twins are born in May or June, their white spots camouflaging them on the forest floor as dappled sunlight. It is an important adaptation, as after birth they are unable to travel for almost ten days. Does leave the fawns for long periods of time returning only to nurse, an act of protection so as not to draw attention to them. The deer population at Acadia is not as high as the island's resources might support. Studies conducted through tracking radio-collared specimens determined deer were healthy and having twins. The majority of mortalities are caused by predators, primarily coyotes and domestic dogs. Coyote scat indicates that deer is their primary food, with raccoons being second.

Prior to 1981, coyotes were not present in Acadia and probably crossed to the island over ice or the bridge, or perhaps by swimming. Radio collaring and howling surveys helped researchers determine that Acadia supports a healthy population of family groups. Red foxes, which share similar habitat as coyotes, appear to live on the edges of each pack's range. The red fox frequent shores and meadows in search of snowshoe hares, white footed mice, meadow voles, and other small rodents, as well as the occasional green crab from the shore. Unfortunately, in past years, red foxes have also turned to people for easy handouts.

The park's wet marshy areas are excellent places to view wildlife, especially at dawn or dusk. Otters can be found playing in lakes and ponds like Witch Hole Pond, while its shores are frequented by species such as mink. At night, bats swoop over unseen bugs, while the nocturnal long-tailed weasel retreats from

its rocky burrows in search of mice, birds, snakes, and chipmunks.

Perhaps the most sought after wetland dweller is the beaver. At the turn of the century trapping pressures exterminated beavers from Mount Desert Island. George B. Dorr, the first park superintendent, reintroduced two pairs. Beavers are fascinating creatures with remarkable adaptations such as waterproof fur, teeth used to ax down trees, webbed feet for swimming, and a flat tail that keeps them from falling over when standing to chew. They are one of the few animals, besides people, to change their environment to suit their needs. A stream lined by birch and aspen, the beaver's preferred food, is the ideal habitat. Within a few days, the beaver transforms the forest into a woodlot and dams the stream to form a pond. A conical lodge built from twigs, mud, and other debris will house the beaver and its family.

Bird life abounds in wetlands too, whether they be pond or marsh. Here the eastern phoebe, with its deep demanding *phee-bee* call, can be found swooping the water's edge catching insects. Joining in across the open water and marshes are the swallows. The barn swallow is distinguished by its V-shaped tail, while the tree swallow is identified by its blue-green back and wings and its

white underbelly. The common yellowthroat warbler's *witchity-witchity-witchity* call can be heard in the marsh and woodland brush while the yellow warbler's *sweet-sweet-sweet* is a common song in the mix. In the deciduous woods, the American redstart, with its bright orange patches on its black wings and tail, is found in the upper levels of the deciduous woods, while the ovenbird, a small little olive-brown warbler, flutters about in the lower levels, building its nest on the forest floor. It's emphatic *teacher-teacher-teacher* call is easy to recognize. Red-eyed vireos, in search of caterpillars and moths, hop from branch to branch.

A good location to find these more southern migrants is around the Sieur de Monts area, with its combination of mixed woods and wetlands. More northern species can be found in the park's conif-

erous forests such as Otter Point, Wonderland, and Ship Harbor. Eighteen species of wood warblers can be found in these areas. The black-throated green warbler, with its bright yellow face, black throat, and greenish back, flits from tree to tree in evergreen forests, calling *zee-zee-zee-zee-zoo-zee*. The blackpoll warbler, another resident of coniferous woods, has a remarkable migration story. It can fly without stopping to its winter home in South America in just about 3-days time. Most of Acadia's birds have traveled well beyond the park's boundaries. Many species considered native head south, crowding into much smaller ranges than their breeding ones in northern areas. Habitat protection is essential beyond our borders so migrant numbers do not decrease.

During autumn, the migration of thousands of hawks takes place. Overhead, especially on Beech and Cadillac mountains, wave after wave can be seen, as kestrals, broad-winged hawks, and sharp-shinned hawks begin their treks to the southern United States, Central America, and South America. On September 15, 1993 a count yielded 671 hawks in a 6-hour period.

Above left: Muskrats either create burrows in the sides of banks, or build mound-shaped lodges from mud and vegetation. Marshy places with an abundance of cattails, a major source of food and building material, are the muskrat's preferred habitat.
Photo by Wayne Lynch

Above right: Raccoon. Primarily nocturnal, these mischievous creatures frequent, in addition to campgrounds, both freshwater and ocean shores in search of food.
Photo by David Middleton

Left: The red fox is slightly smaller than the coyote, with auburn fur, white belly, and black-stockinged legs. Its bushy tail is tipped with white. Although red fox share the same habitat requirements as coyote, their territories remain somewhat separate. Red fox can be prolific beggars in some areas and should not be fed.
Photo by Tim Fitzharris

Winter birds include the American tree swallow, found in thickets, and the year-round resident black-capped chickadee, whose "dee-dee-dee" call rings on cold winter days. Maine's state bird, the chickadee, makes its home in tree cavities, usually dead birch.

Another year round resident is the red-breasted nuthatch, a member of coniferous forests who seems to comically walk down the sides of trees. Its feet, like those of woodpeckers, are adapted for climbing with two toes in front and two in back. Other year-round residents include the downy and the hairy woodpecker; small birds about eight inches in length with a patch of red behind their head. To tell them apart is difficult, but the hairy is a little larger. Their powerful beak excavates tree trunks for nest holes and insects, their hard heads are well adapted to absorb the shock. The large red-headed pileated woodpecker's deep cackling laugh is often heard as much as its loud drilling. Pileated woodpeckers create large square holes, littering the tree's base with large chunks of wood and sawdust. The yellow-bellied sapsucker drills rows of small holes in a tree for sap, leaving the tree trunk to appear body pierced.

Ship Harbor's mudflats, Bass Harbor Marsh, Thompson Island, and the bar to Bar Island are excellent locations to view a wide variety of shorebirds picking and plucking among the grasses and rocks. The great blue heron, with its long, gangly legs, appears almost statue-like, patiently awaiting small fish to swim by. Within moments, the heron dives its sharp spear of a beak into the water, catching the fish. Opportunistic, herons also eat snakes, mice, and mussels. Small sandpipers run back and forth along the mud flats, picking at whatever the tide brings in.

Everywhere along the shore are gulls. The common herring gull has gray wings and back. The great black-backed gull is a larger bird

with black wings and is called the "minister" of the coast. Both have red spots on their bills. These spots serve as visual stimuli for the young, exciting them into a feeding mode which in turn forces the parents to regurgitate food to feed them. Gulls, like most seabirds

Above: Plentiful in Maine, the moose makes rare visits in Acadia, occasionally taking residence in the park's bogs and marshlands. Its large lumbering appearance and drooping snout are distinguishing characteristics. Moose are powerful swimmers, capable of out-swimming two hard-paddling canoeists.
Photo by Jeff Foott

live to be 20 or 30 years old. Immature gulls have a brown mottled

SMALL CREATURES

Acadia, with its wide diversity of environments, offers a haven for many little creatures. Reptiles and amphibians are represented in the park, even though Acadia, because of its cooler northern climate, does not offer the best environment for cold-blooded species.

The park's aquatic and terrestrial habitats harbor salamanders. The common red-backed salamander, recognized by its reddish stripe marking the near entire length of its body, is usually found under leaf litter, rocks, and rotting logs. The spotted salamander, the red-spotted newt, the two-lined salamander, or the more difficult to find, dusky and four-toed salamander inhabit the park's moist environments.

Frogs and toads can be distinguished by a few basic characteristics. Frogs have smooth skin, long legs, webbed feet, and are water

creatures. Toads have dry, bumpy skin, short legs, little or no foot webbing, and are found in both land and water environments. Common Acadia frogs are the square-spotted pickerel frog, the bullfrog, green frog, and spring peeper. The bullfrog's deep-throated jug-a-rum, the banjo "plucking" call of the green frog, and the spring peeper's "peeps" are a common chorus. A male spring peeper can repeat his call about 4,500 times any night!

Reptiles are also present on the island. Five species of non-poisonous snakes are found within the park. The smooth green snake is all green and about one to one and a half feet long. The common garter snake, measuring about two feet long, has mottled coloring that can be black, brown, or olive-green. The milk snake grows up to three feet long and is marked with a black, brown, and white geometric pattern. The ring-necked snake and the red-bellied snake are recognized by the characteristic markings that gave them their distinctive names. The common snapping turtle and the eastern painted turtle also call the park home.

Acadia's insects are everywhere. Critical for the overall health of any habitat, they are important to many of Acadia's bird species, especially during their chicks' growing phase. Some of the more easily recognized insects are the enchanting green luna moths, the

acrobatic damselflies, the curious spittle bugs, or the ever pestering black flies. Also are the wonderful butterflies such as the amazing monarch, the orange sulphur, and the tiger swallowtail.

Left:Spring peeper frog. A chorus of peeps from these thumbnail-size frogs echo throughout Acadia's wetland areas, reaching a full crescendo in May.
Photo by John Shaw

Above: A common resident of ponds and lakeshores, damselflies are voracious predators, scooping up insects in mid-air with their bristly legs. During the 1940's insect inventories were completed and more than 6,500 species and subspecies of insects were found in the Mount Desert Island area. Since then additional species have been discovered.
Photo by John Shaw

appearance that remains for three to four years until sexually mature. Gulls search the shores for sea urchins, mussels, crabs, and

other gourmet delights. To shatter the hard shell exterior, the food is dropped while in flight onto the rocks, leaving shell debris behind. Coastal shores are not the only place gulls find food. Herring gull populations have escalated, taking advantage of garbage dumps and well-meaning people who feed them. Their large population is now a problem since gulls prey on eggs and young of other seabirds. Gulls should not be fed in the park.

Seabirds nest in colonies on ledges and off-shore islands partially to protect against predation. They are mostly monogamous, since two parents are crucial to the development of the nestling whose large appetite requires constant attention. By laying only a few eggs, they are able to concentrate on feeding their young and saving energy for winter months. On the other hand, since they lay few eggs, disturbances within populations of these species can be very disruptive.

It is hard to believe that at the turn of the century gulls and other seabirds were almost extinct. Seaside photographs from this time show a surprising lack of birds. Hunted largely for their eggs, meat, and feathers for the millinery trade, these populations quickly decreased. Wide-scale slaughters and egg collection by the boatload took their toll. One of the very first acts of conservation in this country was seabird protection. The formation of the Audubon Society was just one result. Today seabirds are still protected, although duck hunting is practiced but regulated.

The common eider, whose population numbers in this area were minimal, are now estimated at 30,000 locally. A year-round resident, the male's large black and white body stands out among the waves, while the female's drabber, mottled brown appearance blends in. Come August, males edge closer to the mainland shores, congregating in huge rafts which stretch for hundreds of feet. Here they will spend the winter, rising and falling with the ocean swells, feeding on mollusks. Eiders eat them whole, grinding their shells in their powerful gizzards.

Eiders nest on the same islands as gulls, which seems to be risky business considering gulls prey on eider young. The trade-off is that territorial gulls keep other seabirds away. Females sit on their eggs for 26 to 28 days, leaving them only when threatened, not even for food. Real danger comes after the chicks hatch and head for the water, just 24 hours after being born. Great black-backed gulls swoop down on the vulnerable chicks, picking off up to 50 % of the young. The ducklings that survive are quickly herded in "crêches,"

which consist of a dominant mother and peripheral females. A dominant mother could potentially end up with 12 ducklings in addition to her original four.

The large black birds seen on ledges and rocks with their wings outstretched are the double-crested cormorants. Their characteristic "drying out" stance on land is done for a good reason. The cormorants flap their wings vigorously before diving in the water, releasing as much trapped air as possible. With less trapped air, the feathers will absorb more water, and add more weight for deeper dives after fish. Upon leaving the water, the heavy cormorants drag themselves to the rocks to dry. Cormorants can be differentiated from loons from a distance by their slightly upturned beak, versus the parallel lines of the common loon.

The little black guillemot is another common seabird along the coast. Its cousin, the puffin, is rarely sighted along Acadia's shores. The guillemot's spring and summer plumage of black body and white-patched wings distinguish it from other seabirds. Also called a sea pigeon, it sometimes appears to fly underwater, flapping

Above left: During the summer months, rafts of striking black and white male eider ducks carpet the ocean surface. The mottled brown female eiders congregate in smaller groups close to shore with their ducklings.
Photo by Leonard Lee Rue, III.

Above right: Herring gulls number in the thousands along the shores. A large population increase after near-extinction at the turn of the century is due in part to the herring gull's ability to scavenge, especially from people and garbage dumps. There are concerns over the predatory effect on other seabird colonies, in particular, eider ducks and terns. Gulls are quite large with a wingspan of 4 ½ feet.
Photo by Tim Fitzharris

Left: Rarely seen directly off the Acadia coast, puffins are birds of the open sea. More common to Acadia's shore is the little black and white guillemot, a cousin to the puffin.
Photo by Bill Silliker Jr.

its wings just below the water's surface. It lays its conical-shaped eggs among rocks and ledges, scraping out a space in the gravel.

Nesting along the shorelines are bald eagles and osprey. Osprey nests, made of sticks, vegetation, and anything that can be woven together, are found on tall trees, high cliffs, or any platform. A rather famous nest in the Acadia area is on the side of Sutton Island. For decades, this nest has produced young osprey, as well as many appreciative onlookers. Ospreys, also called fish hawks, are remarkable fishermen. Able to spot a fish swimming near the surface, the osprey dives towards the water, skimming the surface with its talons. Grabbing the fish, the osprey will then turn its flopping prey around in their sandpapery talons so it is aligned and streamlined to their body, making flight easier.

The bald eagles search these waters for fish, but their diet also consists of seabirds. Bald eagles approached near-extinction due to the effects of habitat loss, hunting, and pesticide use, in particular, DDT. In most parts of the country, they have bounced back and are no longer listed as endangered. In Maine however, bald eagle reproduction rates are not as high as in other areas of the country, with an average of less than one chick produced per nest. Studies conducted at Acadia indicate one possible culprit may be the persistence of poly-chlorinated biphenyls (PCB's) and even DDT in Maine's cold, acidic soils.

The peregrine falcon faced a similar situation but fared worse than the bald eagle. The peregrine falcon picks off songbirds in mid-flight, sometimes achieving flight speeds of over 100 mph. As DDT accumulated within the songbird population, it was inevitable that this top predator in the food chain would be greatly affected. In birds of prey, DDT decreased calcium production, critical for the thickness of the eggshells. By the end of the 1960's, peregrines were completely gone from areas east of the Mississippi.

Historically, Acadia had two nesting sites of peregrine falcons; one at Saint Sauveur by Valley Cove in Somes Sound and one at Champlain Mountain. Today they grace Acadia's skies once again due to the efforts of a reintroduction program. From 1984 until 1986 Acadia worked in cooperation with Cornell University and the Peregrine Fund in Boise, Idaho to help bring these birds back to the New England coast.

The chicks, acquired from Cornell, were hand-reared in the lab for the first few weeks of their lives before being transferred to the wild. The young peregrines were placed in a specially equipped box on a high cliff face. Site attendants fed the chicks through a chute in the box, taking care the young did not see them as a food source.

Twenty two of twenty three chicks successfully took flight in a three year period. The hacking project ended when an adult peregrine returned. Monitoring began of the favored cliff, the Precipice trail, along Champlain Mountain. The end result? Nesting pairs on Champlain as well as other mountains in the park.

Acadia's wealth of wildlife is due in part to its varied ecosystem, but also because of the protection afforded these habitats. Habitat loss is the greatest threat to wildlife. Through research, monitoring, and inventorying, park managers better understand the park's ecosystems and potential changes and threats. This, along with the cooperation of the public, greatly enhances all protection efforts.

Above right: The successful reintroduction of peregrine falcons to Acadia resulted in nesting pairs raising young. Look to the skies around Champlain Mountain during the spring and summer to catch a glimpse of this magnificent raptor seeking its song or seabird prey.
Photo by Len Rue Jr.

Above: Drumbeats in the woods? Most likely the rapidly beating wings of a male ruffed grouse.
Photo by Wayne Lynch

Right: The haunting tremolo of a loon across a fog obscured lake creates just one of many unforgettable Acadian moments.
Photo by Wayne Lynch

Marine Mammals

The waters around Acadia National Park are home to 12 different marine mammals. Some, like seals, porpoises, and minke whales, can be seen on boat excursions close to Acadia shores, while other species, such as the humpback whales, and the large finback whales, are better seen on whale-watching trips which venture further off-shore.

Like land mammals, whales and seals are warm blooded, breathe air through lungs, give live birth, and nurse their young. They are also extremely specialized for lives spent either completely in the water or in both an aquatic and terrestrial world. To maintain a stable body core temperature in cold waters, heat retention becomes critical, and is partially accomplished with a thick layer of blubber. Reduced respiration rates and increased metabolism also help to maintain heat.

For life in water, streamlined bodies are a necessity to reduce drag. Even their reproductive organs and mammary glands are internal. Only flippers, and in the case of whales, a dorsal fin and tail fluke, break the svelte lines of these animals. Specialized lungs help them to stay underwater for long periods of time. Some species can stay submerged for up to one or two hours before resurfacing to exhale and take in new air.

Marine mammal senses are well-suited for the demands of their environment. Their sense of smell is limited, although seals are more sensitive to smell because of time spent on land. Taste buds are present although rudimentary. Vision underwater is not particularly good due to dimming light, but different whales and seals have varying degrees of

Harbor seal pup. The waters around Acadia National Park are home to 12 different marine mammals. Generally not sighted from land, seals can be found lounging on offshore rocks and ledges. Harbor seals are very common around Acadia and along the coast of Maine. They are relatively small, reaching lengths of up to 5 feet and a weight of about 200 pounds. They are active and opportunistic feeders and this area of the Gulf of Maine provides plenty of fish, crustaceans, mollusks, and even seabirds to satisfy their appetites.
Photo by Stephen Mullane.

visual abilities primarily used for prey detection, to maintain herd structure for those traveling in groups, and to recognize members of the same species. Seals have particularly good eyesight underwater even at greater depths and, because of their partial life on land, see well above water. Tactile senses are well developed in seals which use the coarse hairs, called vibrissae, situated on their upper lips and above the eyes, to locate prey movement and help them find their way above and under water.

By far, though, the most important sense is hearing. Sound, traveling four times faster and further in water than on land, is used intensively by marine mammals. Vocalization is used for calling or signaling distress. Echolocation is a high frequency, short wavelength sound pulse emitted by whales that reflects back, informing them about an object's size and distance. It is particularly well developed in the toothed whales, especially dolphins. In some species, it may also be used for stunning potential prey to make capture easier.

The fur seals and sea lions, the walruses, and the true seals are all members of the pinniped family (from the Latin meaning wing or feather footed). Around the Mount Desert Island area are found four species of seals: the harbor seal, the gray seal, the harp seal, and the hooded seal. Sometimes seals can be seen directly from the coast, swimming by or resting on rocky outcroppings. The best chance of seeing seals however, requires a boat trip to off-shore ledges. The most common seal around Acadia is the harbor seal. Small, an adult male

Left: White-sided dolphin breaching. Note its distinctive side markings. Very social animals, the white-sided dolphin is often seen in the Gulf of Maine in schools of a few to 500 individuals.
Photo by Stephen Mullane

Right: A humpback whale breaching. Humpback whales are fairly common in this area and can be spotted performing acrobatics such as breaching, rolling, flipper-slapping, and fluking.
Photo by Stephen Mullane

only reaches five feet in length and a weight of about 200 pounds. Females are slightly smaller. Its typical bluish-gray coat with many small dark spots can make it appear tan, brown, black or any color in between. Harbor seals are carnivores, as are all seals, and will be most active during high tides feeding on fish, invertebrates, and even seabirds. Gray seals are much less common than harbor seals in the Acadia area. They are large, with adult males reaching up to 8 feet and weighing about 1,000 pounds, and have an easily recognizable long nose with flaring nostrils. Usually darker than the harbor seal, the coat carries larger and bolder spots and varies in color from gray, to brown, and near black. The harp seal and the hooded seal can also be sighted near Acadia. Although rare they have had increased occurrences during recent winters. The harp seal adult male will reach 6 feet and a weight nearing 300 pounds. Considered beautiful, they have a dark head and are whitish-tan, silver, or even cream with a series of darker markings along the back and flanks forming a saddle, or harp. The hooded seal reaches sizes of eight and a half feet and 800 pounds. They are bluish gray in appearance with a dark camouflage-like pattern on the back, and a black face. The male carries an unmistakable enlarged nasal cavity that, when inflated, forms a hood up to twice the size of a football.

Visitors to Acadia are blessed by the presence near-shore and off-shore of whales. Belonging to the mammalian order cetaceans, all whales, dolphins, and porpoises are divided into two distinct groups: the toothed and baleen whales. Toothed whales are usually under 30 feet and include, among others, porpoises, dolphins, killer whales, and sperm whales. Baleen whales are usually larger than 30 feet and benefit from specialized adaptations for surviving on a diet of plankton and small fish. These include a series of comb-like baleen plates hanging from the upper jaws that form a sieve to filter tiny prey from the water. In the rorqual whale family, including the finback, the humpback, the sei, the blue, and the Bryde's whales, tubes running along the throat and chest assist in feeding. These tubes stretch to accommodate huge amounts of water. Once the whale gulps large volumes of water, the contents are strained out as it squirts the water through its baleens, trapping plankton and small fish inside its mouth which are then ingested. Diets consist of krill, copepods, and other plankton species, as well as fish and squid in some whales, such as the minke. Baleen whales without the charac-

teristic tubes, such as the right whale, constantly filter feed, allowing for the food-rich water to come in and out, while swimming.

Numerous toothed whales inhabit the Gulf of Maine. Often seen around Acadia's bays are harbor porpoises. They are small, about 5 ½ feet in length with a weight of about 140 pounds and can be recognized as they come up to breathe by a small triangular dorsal fin with a rounded tip. When they exhale they will make a soft puff, having no visible spout, which has given them their local name of "puffing pigs." Other features are a dark gray color with lighter flanks, and the absence of a beak. They usually avoid boats under way and are seen individually, in small groups, or in large groups of 20 or more in late summer.

Only found in the north Atlantic, the white-sided dolphin is common offshore from Acadia in the Gulf of Maine, especially in summer and early fall. It is distinguished easily by a narrow white patch followed by a tan or yellow patch on each side from below the dorsal fin to the tail. Fairly large, up to about 9 feet, it is a very social and highly spirited animal. It is often seen in schools, small and large, and in the company of other species of dolphins and larger whales.

The white-beaked dolphin is slightly larger than the white-sided and grows up to 10 feet. Sometimes confused with the white-sided, it has a distinctive white patch on its back, right behind the dorsal fin. On each side, a narrow white stripe reaches the dorsal patch behind the dorsal fin. A distinctive white-grayish to brownish colored snout gives it its name. Only found in the North Atlantic, sightings in the Gulf of Maine are common from May to November.

Widely distributed throughout the oceans of the world is the common dolphin. Smaller, to about 8 feet, they can be observed further off-shore in the Gulf of Maine in groups that can be

Above: Humpback whales primarily feed on small schooling fish such as herring. To herd the fish, humpbacks may stun them by slapping the water or through a flipper visual display underwater. Bubbles released by the whale form a wall to help keep the fish penned, before a surge in the middle of the bubble wall will allow the whales to gulp large amounts of prey .
Photo by Thomas Mark Szelog

Left: Finback whale raising its large fluke prior to another dive near Mount Desert Island. Growing to a size of up to 85 feet in length (26m), it is the second largest whale after the blue whale, which can attain lengths of up to 100 feet. The finback is a member of the rorqual whale family including the minke whale, the Bryde's whale, the humpback whale, the sei whale, and the blue whale.
Photo by Stephen Mullane

quite large. They are fast and acrobatic swimmers and, being social animals, enjoy bow-riding. They are recognizable by a pointed snout and distinctive tan-yellow to gray "hourglass" shaped side pattern.

The bottlenose dolphin, the most popular of all marine mammals and of "Flipper" fame, is more easily seen further south from the Carolinas to south Florida, but will be observed from time to time in the Gulf of Maine and on Georges Bank.

Killer whales are present in the summer months. Their distinctive black and white coloring is easily recognized. They usually travel in pods, mostly made up of relatives, feeding on fish, squid, birds, seals, and even on baleen whales.

Other toothed whales are also seen in the Gulf of Maine but less regularly, such as the white beluga and the largest of all, the

sperm whale. The sperm whale is found in very deep waters, staying at the edge of the continental shelf.

Baleen whales in the Acadia area include the minke, humpback, finback, and northern right. The small minke whale is often seen in Frenchman Bay and the waters off the Cranberry Isles. Reaching about 30 feet in length, they are black to dark-gray on top and white underneath. Although not acrobatic, they are curious and will often approach small boats.

The most acrobatic of whales are the humpbacks. Sometimes seen in Frenchman Bay, they are common to waters around Acadia. They are easy to identify with long flippers, up to a third of body length, knob-like swellings on their head and snout, and the white coloration on the underside of the flukes. Since no two flukes are alike, their shape and coloration help researchers identify and study individual humpbacks. These acrobats show a variety of displays such as breaching, rolling, flipper slapping, and fluking. They are well known for their haunting whale songs. These vocalizations can last for up to 20 minutes. A bushy ten foot spout from its blowhole helps to identify the whale on the horizon before the actual sighting.

Above right: The finback is found in all oceans of the world and is the most common large baleen whale in the Gulf of Maine. Spotted first by its towering spout of up to 20 feet, it is then recognizable by its long body, its tall dorsal fin, and the assymetric white coloration of the right side of its head and lips.
Photo by Tui de Roy

Above: A northern right whale surfaces. These large baleen whales offer one of the most thrilling sights for any whale watcher as they are some of the rarest whales in the world. The callosities on their heads are small amphipods parasites. The right whale has an odd-shaped mouth with huge baleen plates which continuously filter food out of the water as the whale swims.
Photo by Stephen Mullane

Right: This humpback is shown in front of Mount Desert Rock, a rock outcropping 23 miles off the coast of Mount Desert Island. Originally housing a lighthouse keeper and his family, it has also served as a research station on marine mammals.
Photo by Stephen Mullane

Finback whales are the largest whales sighted in this area. They have long narrow bodies which reach a length of up to 85 feet, although the average length is around 65 feet. Their main habitat is the continental shelf, and they are commonly seen offshore of Acadia. They are often spotted by their large 20 foot bushy spout. Finback whales have uneven markings on their snout, showing a dark jaw and baleen on their left side, while on the right side it is light-colored. Biologists theorize that this may help in herding their prey before lunge feeding.

Another regular visitor to the Gulf of Maine is the massive and odd-shaped northern right whale. Growing to a size of 50 feet, it weighs up to an incredible 100 tons, or 220,000 pounds. Hunted to near extinction because of its high yield of blubber, there are only about 350 of them remaining in the western North Atlantic. They can be recognized from afar by their distinctive V-shaped spout. Up close, their slow and fat rounded body with a lack of dorsal fin is unmistakable.

Finbacks, humpbacks, and minkes were at one time hunted from seaports up and down the Maine coast, including from Winter Harbor and Tremont, two towns which border Acadia National Park. Today these creatures and seals are no longer pursued for meat or bounty, but simply for the chance to glimpse one of these magnificent mammals in their natural environment.

White-Sided Dolphin
Lagenorhynchus acutus
size: 7-9 ft (2.1-2.7 m)
Common in the western North Atlantic and in the Gulf of Maine in summer and autumn. Very social, energetic, and acrobatic.

Harbor Porpoise
Phocoena phocoena
size: 4-6 ft (1.2-1.8 m)
Often seen in the Gulf of Maine and around Acadia. Shy, it can be detected on calm days by its "puffing" blow.

Common Dolphin
Delphinus delphis
size: 6-8 ft (1.8-2.4 m)
Widely distributed worldwide, common offshore in the Gulf of Maine. Fast and energetic, they will approach boats and "bow-ride." Can be seen in very large schools of up to 2,000.

Bottlenose Dolphin
Tursiops truncatus
size: 8-12 ft (2.4-3.60 m)
Widely distributed throughout waters worldwide, it prefers temperate and tropical waters. It will be seen occasionally in the Gulf of Maine. Bottlenose are very social and acrobatic.

White-Beaked Dolphin
Lagenorhynchus albirostris
size: 8-10 ft (2.4-3 m)
Less common than white-sided dolphin in the Gulf of Maine. A robust and large dolphin it can also be quite acrobatic.

Beluga
Delphinapterus leucas
size: 9-15 ft (2.7-4.50 m)
Rare in the Gulf of Maine, they are usually observed further north into sub-arctic Canada and off Greenland.

Scale: 1/20 th based on size of mature animals within northern Atlantic range.
All illustrations © Pieter Arend Folkens

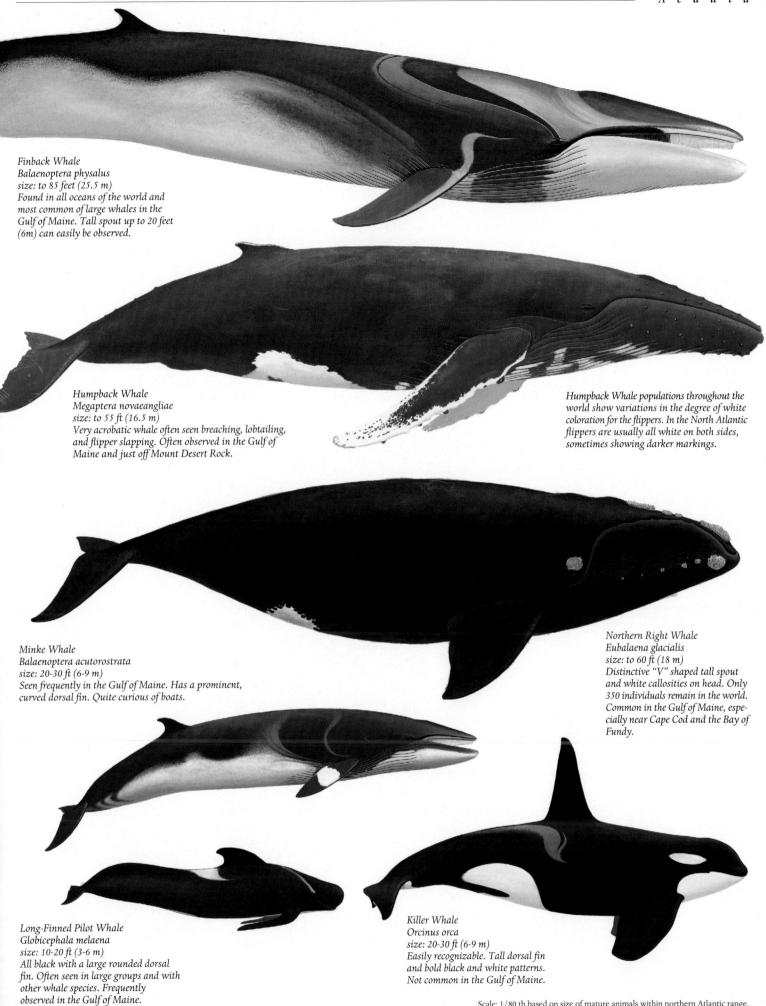

Finback Whale
Balaenoptera physalus
size: to 85 feet (25.5 m)
Found in all oceans of the world and
most common of large whales in the
Gulf of Maine. Tall spout up to 20 feet
(6m) can easily be observed.

Humpback Whale
Megaptera novaeangliae
size: to 55 ft (16.5 m)
Very acrobatic whale often seen breaching, lobtailing,
and flipper slapping. Often observed in the Gulf of
Maine and just off Mount Desert Rock.

Humpback Whale populations throughout the
world show variations in the degree of white
coloration for the flippers. In the North Atlantic
flippers are usually all white on both sides,
sometimes showing darker markings.

Minke Whale
Balaenoptera acutorostrata
size: 20-30 ft (6-9 m)
Seen frequently in the Gulf of Maine. Has a prominent,
curved dorsal fin. Quite curious of boats.

Northern Right Whale
Eubalaena glacialis
size: to 60 ft (18 m)
Distinctive "V" shaped tall spout
and white callosities on head. Only
350 individuals remain in the world.
Common in the Gulf of Maine, especially near Cape Cod and the Bay of
Fundy.

Long-Finned Pilot Whale
Globicephala melaena
size: 10-20 ft (3-6 m)
All black with a large rounded dorsal
fin. Often seen in large groups and with
other whale species. Frequently
observed in the Gulf of Maine.

Killer Whale
Orcinus orca
size: 20-30 ft (6-9 m)
Easily recognizable. Tall dorsal fin
and bold black and white patterns.
Not common in the Gulf of Maine.

Scale: 1 / 80 th based on size of mature animals within northern Atlantic range.

W as it the island's mountains and shores that drew the area's first inhabitants? Probably, although not for their beauty, which indeed made a spectacular backdrop. The predecessors to the more recent Wabanaki were drawn by the natural resources. The earliest evidence of habitation on Mount Desert Island dates back 3,000 years at Fernald Point on Somes Sound. This low sloping land, protected by mountains on either side of the fjord, provided game, blueberry-covered slopes, and access to the water. Low tide exposed mud flats of clams and mussels. Recent excavations uncovered housepit remains and large shell middens. The existence of artifacts from non-local materials implicate trade or exchange between Nova Scotia and inland Maine. Unfortunately, an incomplete story is told due to the constant erosion by the sea and weather. Written records, beginning in the 1500's, describe a more recent people, the Wabanaki, and their encounters with Europeans. Unfortunately, many of these written accounts gave biased opinion of the natives, describing them as an uncivilized and rude people. Others however, were impressed by their disinterest in material goods and the joy they found in life.

The Native Americans already had some contact with Europeans by the time Sieur de Monts and his navigator, Samuel Champlain, were dispatched in 1604 by King Henry IV of France to claim land from the 40th parallel to the 46th. Their expedition settled north of Mount Desert Island at Saint Croix along the Maine/Canadian border. Accompanied by a crew of 12 and two members of the Wabanaki people, Champlain left to further

Gravestones of the Gilley Family on Baker Island.

"To the brave settlers who leveled forests, cleared fields, made paths by land and water and planted commonwealths. To the brave women who in solitude amid strange dangers and heavy toil reared families and made homes."
From: <u>John Gilley, One of the Forgotten Millions</u>
by Charles Eliott
Photo by Glenn Van Nimwegen

scout southward. While mapping the rocky shore they sailed close to Mount Desert Island. Champlain wrote in his journal: *"Setting out from the mouth of St. Croix and sailing westward along the coast, the same day we passed near to an island some four or five leagues long. From this island to the mainland on the north the distance is not more than a 100 paces. It is very high, and notched in places, so that there is the appearance to one at sea, as if seven or eight mountains extending along near each other. The summit of the most of them is destitute of trees, as there are only rocks on them. The woods consist of pines, firs, and birches only. I named it: Isles des Monts Deserts."*

Sieur de Monts was not the first explorer sent by France to sail past this coast. Sixty years prior, Giovanni de Verrazano, an Italian sailor exploring in the name of Francis I, left the northwestern African coast and after seven weeks at sea, reached the North Carolina coast. His voyage continued north towards Newfoundland, most likely passing by the mountainous island. An error in map making named this region "Arcadia," the name Verrazano had actually given to the Carolina coast. The present day name Acadia may be a derivation of this, or it may have come from the French derivation of the Native American word for the area, "La Cadie," meaning "the place."

Sieur de Monts eventually lost his rights to the province of Acadia when Henry IV was dethroned. France, however, had no intention of losing their foothold in the New World. Acadia was then granted to a member of the French aristocracy, Madame de Guerchville.

Left: Bar Harbor as seen from the summit of Cadillac Mountain. Eden, Bar Harbor's original name, was certainly appropriate considering the beautiful view of the town nestled along the shores of Frenchman Bay.
Photo by James Randklev

Right: Sieur de Monts and his navigator Samuel Champlain, travelled in sailing ships not much different from this schooner. They settled Saint Croix Island near the present-day Maine/Canada border. Champlain's scouting mission along the coast resulted in important navigational maps and notes, as well as the naming of a large mountainous island, "Isles des Monts Deserts" or as we know it today: "Mount Desert Island."
Photo by Michael Melford

THE NATIVE AMERICANS

The first people in this region were probably Paleo-Indians who wandered into the area around 11,000 years ago after the last great ice sheet of the Wisconsin Ice Age had retreated north. More than likely following herds of caribou, musk-ox, mammoth, and other large mammals, they slowly adapted themselves to this new land and began to take advantage of both coastal and inland locations.

The earliest evidence of prehistoric people on Mount Desert Island is at Fernald Point, dating back to 1,000 B.C. The south-facing sloping beach at the sound's mouth received the warmth of the sun's rays, while the mountains behind shielded the site from northern winds. Although sea level has since risen and time and erosion have removed some evidence, clues unearthed by archaeologists shed light on these people's lives. The remains of a house pit, relics of clay pots, bowls, and other implements, as well as non-local materials, reveal information about their daily life and their trade connections with other groups. Refuse piles, in the form of shell middens, expose bones from flounder, cod, haddock, as well as bald eagle, great blue heron, porpoise, gray seal, beaver, moose, and the great auk. The large amount of clam shells in these middens yielded information about the seasonality of the Fernald Point site. By examining growth rings from soft-shell clam remains, archaeologists believe that winters, which are milder than inland, were spent along the coast. The encampment then moved inland during summer to take advantage of game and the fish in the rivers.

This same site would be home to the Wabanaki 2,500 years later. The Penobscot, Passamaquoddy, Micmac, and Maliseet make up the four tribes of the Wabanaki. Their estimated population in 1600 A.D. was around 32,000, scattered throughout Maine, New Brunswick, Prince Edward Island, and Nova Scotia. Through hunting, fishing, and plant gathering for sustenance, a balance existed between the natives and the land which supported them. Calling themselves "The People of the Dawn," their view of the land

and animals was one of reverence. Land was not to own, but to have a sacred relationship with. It was believed that animals chose to give up their lives in order for the hunters to live. The hunt was a spiritual journey. Virtually every part of the 60 different animals harvested was used. For example, a moose's sinews became sewing thread, intestines turned into snow-shoe webbing and bow strings, while bones were carved for needles, awls, and spear points. Even the brains were used for tanning hides.

Wigwams were conical or rectangular structures covered with spruce or birch bark; their floors lined with animal skins and fur. The birch bark's amazing resilience, flexibility, and water resistance, made it indispensable for many uses besides wigwams, such as in the making of canoes, bedding, food utensils, and containers.

The Wabanaki tribes were tied to their families and bonds among their members were strong. They were a community prepared to move with the seasons. Larger community groups had leaders called sakoms (zah-q'om), who provided insight and clarity to problems, but group consensus was the basis for decisions. Confrontations did occur among tribes, but alliances were struck as well.

With a deep understanding of life and the joy that could be found in every day, their wealth was not in material possessions but in spiritual matters and the relationships among their family, tribe's people, and the environment around them. Father Christian Le Clercq, a Jesuit priest, noted: "I should consider these Indians incomparably more fortunate than ourselves... for, after all, their lives are not vexed by a thousand annoyances as are ours."

After European arrival, the Wabanaki's lives drastically changed. Demand on land resources magnified with the European's desire for beaver pelts and lumber. Alcohol was often used by unscrupulous traders to take advantage of the Wabanaki. But by far the most disastrous impact was the quick and rampant spread of European diseases. Diseases that many Europeans had built up a resistance to such as chicken pox, measles, pneumonia, influenza, hepatitis, dysentery, bubonic plague, and small pox raced through the native population. Between

1611 and 1613, 75 % of the tribal populations were killed. Further south in Massachusetts, up to 95 % of the natives were wiped out.

Not only did the Wabanaki die, so did some of their beliefs and connections to other tribal communities. Their weakened

state would be exploited by the European's thirst for expansion. The French, at the very least, acknowledged native rights by requiring Native American permission for land acquisition. The English, on the other hand, settled the land and then required people to purchase it or acquire it by deed. The Native Americans, which had neither capability, lost their land, parcel by parcel, treaty by treaty.

The treaties signed were often misunderstood by both sides. To the Wabanakis, who did not understand land ownership, treaties gave the English the right to share the land. The English believed that all rights were terminated and could not understand why the Wabanaki remained on the land. Decade after decade, more and more land disappeared from the Wabanaki and by the end of the 1800's they were stripped of almost all of their original lands, except for what would become their reservations.

On Mount Desert Island, groups were scattered about the island, including in the current ballfield of Bar Harbor and along West Street. The latter encampment became a popular destination for Bar Harbor visitors who would purchase baskets made from sweet grass and birch bark, moccasins, and seal skins. As island development grew, the remaining population dwindled until the land they and their ancestors had known for millenniums no longer welcomed them.

To learn more about the Native Americans of this area, both historic and current, the Robert Abbe Museum located at Sieur de Monts Springs and in Bar Harbor offers an excellent starting place.

Above: The Wabanaki, who began losing their lands upon the arrival of the Europeans, had an encampment on what is today the Bar Harbor ballfield.(c. mid 1880's)

Left: Clark Point in Southwest Harbor. Both the Penobscot and Passamaquoddy tribes lived in this area. Today they live on a reservation in northern Maine. (c. mid 1880's)
Photos courtesy Robert Abbe Museum

Her vision for the area included a Jesuit encampment. The Jesuits moved south after landing at Port Royal on the Annapolis River. Their planned destination was present-day Bangor. Unfavorable weather conditions, namely fog, deterred the group from their original intent. Instead they landed in a beautiful harbor on Mount Desert Island, naming it Saint Sauveur. Historical notes report that they soon moved to present-day Fernald Point, apparently at the request of the natives wishing for them to visit their leader who feigned illness. The Jesuits, impressed by the location at the mouth of Somes Sound, set up their new camp in 1613.

Because North America was a *"new"* world, both the British and French laid claim from the Carolinas to Nova Scotia. The British, determined not to allow colonization by any other power, dispatched Jamestown's Captain Samuel Argall to try to prevent any French settlements. As Argall and his crew searched the coast north of Virginia, they learned of the Jesuits' colony. Upon arrival in the vicinity, a group of natives greeted the boat, telling the English where their *"friends"* lived. The Jesuits, surprised by the attack, fell victim quickly. Argall destroyed the camp, taking some Jesuit prisoners back to Virginia.

Intermittent warfare between the French and English lasted for the next 150 years. This area's role was mostly peripheral, with Frenchman Bay and other harbors serving as a staging ground during the four wars between the French and British. Man O' War Brook in Somes Sound was used as a fresh water supply source for ships.

It wasn't until the final war, The French and Indian War of 1754-1763, that the English won victory and real settlement could begin.

Few incidents were notable during this 150 year period. In 1688, a self-proclaimed nobleman, Antoine Lamuet, received from the

French crown a land grant in the new world that included Mount Desert Island. His visit here was short. Moving further west, he settled in present day Michigan and founded the city of Detroit. Antoine Lamuet is much better known by the title he bestowed upon himself: *"Sieur de la Mothe Cadillac."* Today, the highest mountain in Acadia bears his title, as well as a brand of luxury cars. Another event took place, according to local lore, in 1739 when a ship bound for Philadelphia from Ireland wrecked off the Mount Desert coast. Although the 200 passengers escaped with the cargo, only a handful survived the winter as starvation, disease, and exposure took their toll.

With the French and English skirmishes finally resolved in 1759, Mount Desert Island fell to Sir Francis Bernard, the last royal governor of Massachusetts. Bernard's land acquisition was, in part, a return of a political favor for the personal funds he expended in remodeling the governor's mansion in Boston. This land grant, along with others, ensured Massachusetts claims of land to the north, which included what would become Maine.

Bernard sought settlers, offering them free land to settle on Mount Desert Island. In 1761, James Richardson and Abraham Somes took Bernard up on his land offer, settling a protected harbor between the mountains. The settlement, *"Betwixt the Hills"* would later take on Somes' name as Somesville. At the end of the American Revolution,

Above left: During the 1800's schooners hauled Maine products and resources up and down the Eastern Seaboard and all over the globe.
Above right: Drying fish on Little Cranberry Island in the 1880's. Samuel Hadlock's original store is in the center, the newer, 1850 store to the right. Later acquired and renamed the Blue Duck by William Otis Sawtelle, it served as a museum preserving the island stories until the brick Islesford Historical Museum was built.
Photos courtesy National Park Service

Below: Bar Harbor during the hotel era in the late 1880's. Bar Harbor had 17 hotels to house the ever-increasing seasonal visitors. Four steamers a week docked in Bar Harbor in the late 1800's. The Rodick House, the largest hotel, centered in the photo, grew from a small cottage guest house in 1866, to a massive structure of 400 rooms in 1881. It was demolished in 1906 after the decline of the hotel era. The Reading Room, site of today's Bar Harbor Inn, can be seen just to the left of the town dock.
Photo courtesy Bar Harbor Historical Society

Bernard left for England, his loyalties still with the crown. His son however, did not share his sentiments and remained in America. His request for his father's land grant resulted in his acquisition of the western half of Mount Desert Island. Petitioning for the other half

was Cadillac's grand daughter, Madame de Gregoire. Holding letters from Lafayette and others, the Massachusetts general court honored the request. She and her family settled near Hull's Cove. Almost all land deeds on the island can be traced back to Bernard and Gregoire and the two initial parties that purchased land from them.

In 1820, the year Maine became a state, no longer a part of Massachusetts, the island census showed 2,000 residents. Primarily fishermen and farmers, these everyday citizens constituted the backbone of a new nation, and contributed to its growth. Acadia's Baker Island and the Carroll Homestead in Southwest Harbor, preserve the stories of two families in the 1800's. Their lives help give perspective to the larger historical context.

Seafaring, and its associated occupations, defined coastal Maine throughout the 1800's. A list of occupations documented in the Cranberry Isles census paints a clear picture of the seafaring ties of these people: sea captain, mariner, surfman, shipwright, keeper of light. The Hadlock family, who lived on Little Cranberry Island, represents a cross-section of these trades, including a Civil War captain and an overseas adventurer thrown in for good measure. With prof-

its from an overseas voyage, the first Hadlock store was built in the early 1800's supplying wares for fishing, boat building, and sailing. The operation was later enlarged in 1850 and eventually became a general store. The ledgers and logs found in the Hadlock Ship's Store tell tales of trade from around the world.

The establishment was eventually purchased by summer resident William Otis Sawtelle in the early 1900's. Sawtelle was fascinated by, and committed to, preserving the maritime heritage of the building and the artifacts, ship diaries, logs, and store ledgers found within. Today that collection is housed in the Islesford Historical Museum.

Islands like the Cranberries were prime real estate then, but not because of their scenic views. Lying closer to important shipping routes, still powered by sail, islands were the location of choice by sea captains, traders, and fishermen alike. In fact, two busy and productive fishing communities in Maine were off the Mount Desert Island coast: the Cranberry Isles and Southwest Harbor. Fishing boats headed for Labrador or the Grand Banks, or ships returning from Europe or the West Indies were a common sight. At one time 85 ships called these harbors their home port. During the 1800's, island communities like the Cranberry Isles transported food and other items to growing cities such as Philadelphia, Boston, and New York. The commerce and trade of hearty islanders boosted the economic growth of the Maine coast and the entire Eastern Seaboard as lumber, granite, fish, ice, feathers, and other commodities were distributed to all corners of the globe.

Lighthouses are an integral piece of Maine's nautical history. Today, its 65 lighthouses are all automated. Their lights continue to guide ships around dangerous rocks, show the way to points of land, and alert seaman to narrow harbor entrances. Built in 1828, Baker Island Light was the first in the area. Bass Harbor Light, built in 1858, provides a beacon at the entrance to Bass Harbor and Blue Hill Bay. Egg Rock Light marks a rocky ledge in Frenchman Bay. Built in 1876, the short light tower is accompanied by a fog horn. Bear Island Light, at the entrance to Northeast Harbor, sits high atop the cliff-laced Bear Island. Built

Above left: The Turrets, built in 1893 for John J. Emery. This summer "cottage" cost $100,000 to build. Its granite blocks were cut from a quarry near Eagle Lake. It escaped the fire of 1947 and today is part of the College of the Atlantic.
Photo courtesy Bar Harbor Historical Society

Above: Early hiking party enjoying the mountain views. The island's trail system was well established before the formation of Acadia National Park.

Left: George B. Dorr was the driving force behind the creation of the first national park east of the Mississippi. Concerned by the increasing rate of development on the island, Dorr along with Charles W. Eliot, President of Harvard University, and the Hancock County Trustees of Public Reservations, acquired parcels of land to be preserved for the public's use.
Photos courtesy National Park Service

THE CARRIAGE ROADS

The avenue to many Acadian treasures is found via the carriage roads, an accomplishment of philanthropist John D. Rockefeller, Jr. in the first half of this century. A summer resident of Seal Harbor, he loved the beauty

and unspoiled nature of Mount Desert Island.

Two events would spur Rockefeller, Jr. into his carriage road project. One was his love of the process. He had inherited his father's interest of building carriage roads, which the senior Rockefeller directed at their homes in New York and Ohio. Second, was the inevitable admission of automobiles on the island. Prior to 1913, each town had a local option law, allowing the communities to vote on the presence of the internal-combustion machine. Southwest Harbor and Tremont residents, wishing to partake in the new invention, allowed them. Bar Harbor and the town of Mount Desert (Northeast Harbor, Seal Harbor, and Somesville) with their large summer populations, chose otherwise. For the wealthy, the automobile was part of the hectic city life that they were escaping.

Progress marched on however, and once it appeared that automobiles would ultimately be allowed, Rockefeller, Jr.'s solution was a network of carriage roads. The roads would preserve the horse and carriage lifestyle he enjoyed and eventually provide access into the heart of the island. Beginning in 1913 on

Above: John D. Rockefeller Jr.'s generosity resulted in a gift of 45 miles of carriage roads to Acadia National Park, as well as over 11,000 acres of land.
Image courtesy of Rockefeller Archive Center

Above right: The Jordan Pond Gate House was designed, as the Brown Mountain Gate House, by Grosvenor Atterbury, a New York architect who had already worked on John D. Rockefeller, Jr.'s estate in Tarrytown. The style used is reminiscent of traditional French architecture.
Photo by Jeff Foott

Right: Brown Mountain Stone Gate. Completed in 1932, it was built, as was the Jordan Pond Gate, to monitor the entrance to the carriage road system and to ensure that no automobiles would enter.
Photo by Jeff Gnass

his own property, the system would grow to 57 miles and would become a centerpiece of Acadia National Park.

Rockefeller, Jr. was actively involved in all aspects of design and construction. He was well qualified to take on such a project, with his passion for road building and his well-trained eye for both grand and subtle beauty. It was noted that *".. he knows intimately the physical geography of Mount Desert Island. Its hills, its shorelines, its streams, its woods, where the fine views are, where the autumn colors are best."*

All of these were taken into consideration in the design of the system. Carriage roads wind past ponds and through marshes, wander among stands of spruce, hemlock, and beech, or skirt along the bases of mountains before climbing for panoramic views. A curve in the road delivers a mountain view, while another turn affords a glimpse of the ocean.

The scenery encompassed by the roads is breathtaking, but is only one part of many outstanding features. The roads are state of the art, a combination of machinery and hand labor, built to meet the highest standards. These are true roads, the finest example of broken stone roads in existence today. The foundation consists of four-inch diameter stones laid to a depth of six to seven inches. The second layer is made of two-inch diameter stones laid to a depth of four inches. Fine gravel and a binding material form the hard surface. An eight inch crown, drainage ditches, and culverts were designed to fight erosion.

Details were not overlooked. Sixteen stone bridges, each with their own unique character, blend in with the surrounding environment. At Jordan Stream, a single arch bridge built of cobblestones mirrors the flow of the stream. At Duck Brook, an immense cut-granite, three-arch bridge provides views to Frenchman Bay and Cadillac

Mountain. Another finishing touch was the French Romanesque-style gatehouses located at Jordan Pond and Brown Mountain. Although they never housed a true gatekeeper, they were placed strategically at connections between automobile and carriage roads. Coping stones, known as Rockefeller's teeth, lined the roadways.

Windows to spectacular and modest views were framed with appropriate plantings suggested by landscape architects, in particular, Beatrix Farrand.

By 1940, 27 years after the roads' inception, Rockefeller's vision was realized. Although the roads were complete, the work required to maintain them was endless. Rockefeller, Jr. continued to provide funds and a crew of up to 100 workers to clear debris and keep the roads graded. After his death in 1960, maintenance was turned over to the National Park Service. In 1989, a historic resource study was completed and recommendations to restore the roads and many vistas to their original state were made. Acadia embarked on a major rehabilitation of the system, resulting in a return of the roads' original condition.

in 1839, its fogbell was operated by weights and rang every 15 seconds. Lighthouse keepers without automatic bells would manually ring bells until conditions were safe.

While the local families were arduously tending to their day to day lives, a change was progressively taking place amidst their surroundings. During the 1840's, the first visitors ventured to Mount Desert Island. Artists, writers, scientists, and clergymen sought refuge there from the hectic pace of fast growing East Coast cities.

Thomas Cole, a landscape painter and head of the Hudson River School, was part of this generation interested in pursuing ideals of beauty and romance. Cole's first visit resulted in panoramic paintings done largely from memory. They had a hazy, dreamy quality and caught Acadia's essence. Frederick Church, one of Cole's students, became an avid lover of the island and brought friends with him to share in the splendor. Artists came eager to fill their sketchbooks with crashing surf, eagles soaring above lakes, the mountain cliffs, and the islands of Frenchman Bay. As they sketched, they named what their pencils drew, such as Echo Lake, the Beehive, and Eagle Lake. The paintings which evolved from those sketches tempted those in the cities to discover these magical places. They evoked an appreciation of what nature offered: peace, spirit, introspection, and a soothing balm for the human conscience. Writer's prose generated interest in the islands as well. One travel writer, wrote: *"These mountains are the bones of the earth, which, being broken and upheaved, form some of our most striking and beautiful scenery, giving us lovely valleys, wild mountain passes and sparkling fresh-water lakes, within the sound of the murmuring sea."*

The paintings coupled with poetic imagery lured many to Mount Desert Island. The first steamers to the island brought these visitors, now called *"rusticators,"* to Southwest Harbor. Buckboards carried them throughout the island. They took up residence with farmers and fishermen willing to provide board in their rustic homes. The extra income was welcome, but by 1865, space and hospitality were running out.

To accommodate the increasing number of tourists, many hotels sprung up and island towns developed rapidly. At the height of the hotel era in 1887, there were 17 hotels in Bar Harbor, including the Summit House on Green Mountain (Cadillac), 2 at Seal Harbor, 5 at Northeast Harbor, 6 at Southwest Harbor, one at Islesford, and 3 at

Somesville. Some hotels were very large, such as the Rodick House which could accommodate 600 people and had a two year reservation wait. Although large, it was far from opulent. The beds were stuffed with cornhusks and the food, well in the words of one critic, *"... people that eat and cook food of this wretched description, must have something wrong in their moral condition."* Typhoid broke out in Bar Harbor due to unclean wells, yet people still came. Even if the food was unpalatable and the accommodations uncomfortable, there was food for the soul in the island's cliffs, mountains, and surf.

A summer day's outing to Jordan Pond might include a steamer excursion across Eagle Lake, a hike around the Bubbles, and a row to reach the Pond House. Attractions such as the Green Mountain Cog Railroad, built in 1882, took visitors to the summit of the highest mountain. Common pastimes included *"rocking"* where young ladies and gentlemen, dressed in fancy clothes, would roam the shores, rattling off Latin names of the plants and animals surrounding them. Carriage drives to Spouting Horn (Thunder Hole) took them along the ocean. It was noted that Bar Harbor's summer elite had a *"... vigorous, healthy, sensible feeling in all they do and are not a bit of the overdressed, pretentious, nonsensical, unhealthy sentimentality which may be found at other places (like Long Island and Newport)."* Two of the original hotels, the Claremont in Southwest Harbor and the Asticou in Northeast Harbor, still stand and operate as hotels today.

Some folks, not content to stay in hotels

Above left: Jesup Path in the spring. Part of this trail was already used hundreds of years ago by Mount Desert Island's native Indian tribes. It offers the hiker a true walk back in history.
Photo by Glenn Van Nimwegen

Above: Designed by Charles Stoughton, the Amphitheater Bridge was completed in 1931.
Photo by Willard Clay

Left: Bubble Pond Bridge was built in 1928. Each of the stone bridges of the carriage road network took about one year to complete.
Photo by Jeff Gnass

anymore, purchased property and built *"cottages,"* a rather pretentious term for mansions with up to 80 rooms. The Bar Harbor shores, turned into *"Millionaire's Row,"* while Northeast Harbor became *"Philly on the Rocks"* since so many residents were from Philadelphia. Set in the midst of manicured lawns, many of these spectacular homes were hidden from public view by dense forests. Kenarden, home to the Kennedys, cost over $ 200,000 to build and had its own private electric plant. Wingwood, home to the Stokesburys, had 80 rooms and 28 bathrooms with gold fixtures. Landscaping was a never-ending process, as plants were shifted every two weeks to maintain a continuous bloom. Bar Harbor and Mount Desert Island replaced Newport, Rhode Island, as *"the"* place to summer if you were *"anybody."* The names of those coming to the island were an aristocratic who's who: the Kennedys, Astors, Carnegies, Pulitzers, Vanderbilts, Morgans, and Rockefellers.

The outdoor nature of an earlier time still held on, but activities definitely began to change. Canoe clubs changed to swimming pools, while *"rocking"* and nature walks took second place to parties, tournaments, and horse shows. Social obligations were so numerous that some cottagers actually built *"camps"* to get away from the frantic pace.

The character was changing, and while to many of the summer residents, it passed unnoticed, others became concerned that over-development would forever change the nature of the island they loved. Three men in particular were instrumental in the conception and effort to preserve as much of the island as possible. Charles Eliot, George B. Dorr, and John D. Rockefeller, Jr. would combine their hard work, influence, and wealth to protect the island's beauty in perpetuity for all.

Charles Eliot, president of Harvard University from 1869 to 1909,

whose family had spent summers on Mount Desert Island, took up the cause partially due to his son, Charles Jr.. Charles Jr. returned to the island as a young man with a group of friends and Harvard professors and formed the Champlain Society, a group dedicated to the knowledge and exploration of the island, but also to its preservation. Charles Jr., a landscape architect with the firm of Frederick Law Olmstead noted: *"... can nothing be done, to preserve for the use and enjoyment of the great unorganized body of the common people, some fine parts, at least, of this seaside wilderness of Maine?."* He never saw that question answered, as he died suddenly at the age of 38. His heartbroken father decided to carry forth his son's ideals, and in 1901 he called on the leaders of the island's Village Improvement Societies to consider setting aside lands. These groups already maintained miles of hiking trails through the island's mountains and shores.

Eliot formed the Hancock County Trustees of Public Reservations which was made up of ministers, scientists, and summer residents from Seal and Northeast Harbor along with George B. Dorr, George Vanderbilt, and John S. Kennedy. Although they all played an important role in the preservation of the island, it was Dorr who would carry it to Washington D.C. seeking national park status.

Dorr's family cottage sat on a property extending from Frenchman Bay to the slopes of Newport (Champlain) Mountain. Their family fortune, which came from the East India trade and the textile industry, assured him that he need not work for a living. It was in Dorr's love of the island that he would find his true vocation.

When Eliot asked for his help, Dorr was ready. The threat of the new portable sawmill (chainsaw), the ability for many to descend upon the island, and the purchase of vast tracks of land for private use by wealthy land owners were all serious concerns.

Above: Baker Island Light is located on Baker Island which is owned by the National Park Service. Built in 1828 it is still in service and helps navigation towards Mount Desert Island and Somes Sound.
Photo by Glenn Van Nimwegen

Below: Lobster boats in Bass Harbor. The harbors of Acadia's surrounding communities each have their own distinctive personalities, but lobster boats are common to all.
Photo by James Randklev

It was ironic of course, that Dorr and Eliot, along with other well-to-do members of the Trustees, were to be a part of the solution of slowing the rampant development of the island that

they, all wealthy land owners, had contributed to. George B. Dorr reacted to the challenge with enormous energy. The first land donation made to the Trustees was a small 272 square foot section in Seal Harbor, just large enough for a plaque commemorating Champlain. Donations grew, both in size and number, and by 1913, 5,000 acres were in the Trustees hands.

Also, word came that year that the Trustees tax-exempt status might be in jeopardy. Dorr looked to Washington as a way to assure permanency in preservation of the land that he and the Trustees were trying to protect. Would it be possible for this to be a national park? Dorr received a positive response in Washington and returned to the island to clarify land deeds and purchase more land. Unable to take on the entire financial burden, Dorr turned to Eliot. Eliot then approached John D. Rockefeller, Jr., who had been a summer resident in Seal Harbor since 1910. Rockefeller, Jr., having inherited enormous wealth from his family's oil empire,

gladly donated a substantial monetary gift to continue the efforts.

Dorr spent two years traveling back and forth between the island, Boston, and Washington. Sentiment for the proposed park was not high at first, as Congress hesitated to give money for what they considered a *"rich man's park."* Secretary Lane of the Department of the Interior, working to create a National Park Service to oversee the parks, encouraged Dorr despite the opposition of Congress. Dorr

continued to petition for a national park, arguing that there was a need *"to provide for ... people of moderate or narrow means who would appreciate what it has to give in beauty, interest and climate."*

Lane then proposed that the land tract should become a national monument instead of a park. The president could sign a monument into being, whereas it would take an act of Congress to make it a national park. On July 8, 1916, Sieur de Monts National Monument was formed. The park's charter stipulated that no federal money be spent to purchase land. The park could only grow through land donations. Dorr was appointed custodian with a salary of $1.00 a month. In 1919, it became Lafayette National Park and in 1929, at the request of the English donors of the 2,000 acre Schoodic Peninsula, became

Above left: The Park Loop Road was designed to take advantage of Acadia's many beautiful views, leading visitors from some of the most beautiful rocky shoreline in the country to the majestic views offered from Cadillac Mountain.
Photo by Jeff Gnass

Above: Cottage bridge in Somesville. Somesville was settled at the northern end

of Somes Sound, the only natural "fjord" on the East Coast.
Photo by James Randklev

Below: Considered quieter than its sister Bar Harbor on the island's east side, Southwest Harbor is home to a world renown boat building industry.
Photo by Matti Majorin

Acadia National Park. After Eliot's death, Rockefeller and Dorr continued to work in partnership to acquire land. Rockefeller's instrumental role in land donation resulted in 11,000 acres with carriage roads in place. The Park Loop Road and the drive up Cadillac were also a product of the collaboration between Dorr, Rockefeller, Jr., and Frederick Law Olmstead, Jr.. The road was not developed to get from one point to the next, but to coincide with the natural lay of the land, enhancing views of its beauty for the traveler.

Prior to 1916, the island already had an outstanding trail system in place and it continued to grow in the new national park. Paths from Native Americans, crossings and drives between farms, and logging roads became the initial trails of the island. Adventurous souls in the 1800's and early 1900's blazed new trails, always searching for the best views, with the least damage to the resource.

Many of these trail-building expeditions were directed by each community's Village Improvement Society. Once the park was in existence, their trails were maintained and added to. The Civilian Conservation Corp in the 1930's did a substantial amount of trail building. Today there are more than 115 miles of maintained hiking trails in Acadia National Park.

George B. Dorr died in 1944, having exhausted his family fortune and personal funds. He had contributed much to this national park, including his family's lands. His energy and dedication resulted in this first national park east of the Mississippi, a true gift to the American public. Rockefeller Jr., who died in 1960, also left a legacy of preservation. Not only was he involved in the preservation of Acadia, but other national parks, such as the Blue Ridge Parkway, Great Smoky Mountains, Shenandoah, Grand Teton, and Mesa Verde also benefited from his great generosity and vision.

Other events besides the park's creation changed the character of life on the island. The introduction of the income tax in 1913, the stock market crash of 1929 and the ensuing depression, WWI and WWII, and as a final blow, the fire of 1947, ended the opulent Cottage Era. The fire on Mount Desert Island was just one of thousands that spread across Maine in 1947 spurring the name *"the year Maine burned."* On October 17, a fire at a town dump near Hull's Cove, which was thought to be put out, sprung back to life. Fueled by high winds, it quickly devoured 17,000

acres in less than a week and burned more than half of Bar Harbor, including 237 houses and more than 70 of the glorious cottages. Many of the cottages that burned for good were already in disrepair, their owners having long left them, unable to maintain their upkeep. The land, though, would rebound from the devastating fire with a lush forest of birch and aspen.

The legacy of Acadia National Park is the product of the vision of a privileged few and the hard work of many more. Acadia is a park for all to enjoy. Three million visitors annually trek to this small national park for their chance to pursue magnificent mountain views, spruce forest spires, still lakes, and sea air.

Above right: The Harding's fishing wharf in Bass Harbor. Dedicated to the lobstermen Charles, Bill, and Clarence Harding who departed from this wharf for over 50 years to fish the nearby waters. The lobster buoys hanging from the wall display the licensed colors of their owners.
Photo by Dianne Dietrich Leis

Above: The triple-arch Duck Brook Bridge was completed in 1929 and was built of rough cut granite. From the bridge's turrets are views to both Frenchman Bay and Cadillac Mountain.
Photo by Jeff Foott

Right: Called "Philly on the Rocks" in the late 1800's because of the large number of Philadelphia residents that summered here, today Northeast Harbor and neighboring Seal Harbor contain many older "cottages."
Photo by Jeff Gnass

ACADIA QUICK FACTS

Date Established:
- July 8, 1916: Sieur de Monts National Mnmt.
- February 26, 1919: Lafayette National Park.
- January 19, 1929: Acadia National Park.

Location and Area:
Acadia is the fifth smallest national park. Most of Acadia National Park is located on Mount Desert Island (MDI). Also preserves seven other islands including Isle au Haut and the Schoodic Peninsula. Acadia holds over 46,000 acres.
- 30,300 acres on MDI.
- 2,728 acres on Isle au Haut.
- 2,194 acres on Schoodic Peninsula.
- 10,452 acres in conservation easements.
- 1,110 other.

Features:
- Park Loop Road, made of 27 miles of paved road, carries visitors through some of the most

marine mammals, amphibians, and reptiles. More than 270 species of birds will frequent Acadia's skies throughout the year.

Weather:
Ever changing weather influenced by coastal location. Gulf of Maine waters warm the area in winter and cool it during the summer.
Average winter temperature: 27 degrees
Average summer temperature: 67 degrees
Average annual precipitation: 48 inches
Spring is often damp and cool. Summer can bring days of fog followed by brilliant sunshine. The high temperatures in July and August usually range between 70°F and 80°F. Autumn is a wonderful time to visit with crowds lessening and weather usually crisp and clear. Peak foliage colors usually occur in the first two weeks of October. Winters are often charac-

centers. It provides listings of ranger-led programs such as hikes, walks, evening programs, boat cruises, and children's programs as well as other helpful tips about a visit to Acadia.

Accessibility:
The park provides accessible facilities in some areas, including campsites, restrooms, and trails. The Park Service publishes a guidebook for accessibility available at information centers.

For More Information:
Park Headquarters, P.O. Box 177, Bar Harbor, ME 04609. Phone: (207) 288-3338. Internet: **www.nps.gov/acad/home.htm**
Bar Harbor Chamber of Commerce, P.O. Box 158, Bar Harbor, ME 04609, (207) 288-5103.
Eastern National, a non-profit cooperating association manages book sales in the park. P.O. Box 177, Bar Harbor, ME 04609. (207) 288-4988.

beautiful features of the park and includes a 14.5-mile one-way section. The road travels along the coast, to Sand Beach, to Otter Cliffs, through woods, and to the top of Cadillac Mountain with its amazing views of the coast.
- Acadia has more than 115 miles of maintained hiking trails.
- Over 45 miles of historic carriage roads in the park reserved for hikers, bikers, and horseback riders. Motorized vehicles not permitted.

Geography:
- 26 mountains: Eight mountains over 1,000 feet. *Cadillac*, 1,530; tallest geographic feature of Atlantic Coast north of Rio de Janeiro. *Sargent*, 1,373. *Dorr*, 1,270. *Pemetic*, 1,248. *Penobscot*, 1,194. *Bernard*, 1,071. *Champlain*, 1,058. *Gilmore*, 1,036.
- Somes Sound: Only "fjord" of U.S. East Coast.
- 26 lakes and ponds on MDI. Deepest lake is Jordan Pond with a depth of 150 feet.

Flora and Fauna:
More than 1,000 species of flowering plants meet in an intricate blend of the northern coniferous forest and the temperate deciduous forest. Salt marshes, ponds, meadows, bald granite mountain summits, and a rugged coastline all contribute to an environment harboring nearly 80 species of terrestrial and

terized by periods of snow and rain, and occasional periods of sub-zero temperatures. Visitors should dress in layers and be prepared for a quick change in weather.

General Information:
The park is open year-round. Some park roads are closed during winter. Entrance fees are collected on the Park Loop Road.

Camping and Campgrounds:
Camping is allowed only in designated campsites available at Seawall and Blackwoods on MDI and at Duck Harbor on Isle au Haut. Reservations accepted for Blackwoods and required for Isle au Haut. Overnight backpacking trips prohibited. Pets are allowed but must be on leash and attended.

Park Information Centers:
Hulls Cove Visitor Center is located 1 ½ miles north of Bar Harbor. Open from mid-April to October 31. Hours vary. In winter, Park Headquarters serves as main information center. It is located on Route 233, 3 miles west of Bar Harbor and is open from November through April. Hours : 8:00 a.m-4:30 p.m.. Closed major holidays. Other information centers include Thompson Island and the Sieur de Monts Nature Center. The park's newspaper, *The Beaver Log*, can be picked up at information

Acadia Corporation, operating under contract from the NPS, the Acadia Corporation operates the three gift shops found in the park at Thunder Hole, Jordan Pond, and Cadillac Summit, and has serviced the Jordan Pond House restaurant since 1947. (207) 288-5592.

Museums: Sieur De Monts Spring Area.
The Robert Abbe Museum: This museum contains a very explicit collection of displays on Native American life in and around Acadia.
The Nature Center: Contains exhibits on the natural history of the park.
Wild Gardens of Acadia: Harbors labeled trees and plants aiding identification in the park.

Little Cranberry Island: Islesford Historical Museum: Has informative exhibits on Maine's maritime history.

All information valid as of press time. As information may be subject to change, please contact the National Park Service and their offices on MDI or its web site. Also check Elanpublishing.com for additional links and info.

Above: The scenic drive along the ocean towards Sand Beach and Great Head.
Photo by John Shaw

Right: The coast looking to Otter Cliffs.
Photo by Jeff Gnass

Back cover: Granite monolith in Monument Cove faces the constant onslaught of the ocean.
Photo by William H. Johnson

ACKNOWLEDGEMENTS:

The author wishes to thank the staff of Acadia National Park, especially Deborah Wade, Kristen Britain, Wanda Moran, Shirley Beccue, Kate Petrie, Narissa Willever, Bryant Woods, Brooke Childrey, and Tom Vining, and Becky Cole of the Robert Abbe Museum, and Stephen Mullane of Whalesback Designs. In addition, gratitude to my family for their assistance and to the never-ending wonder of Acadia National Park for its inspiration.